THE SECRET OF A CLEAR HEAD

THE SECRET OF A CLEAR HEAD

BY

J. MORTIMER GRANVILLE

Sixth Thousand

GYAN

Published by

GYAN

Gyan Publishing House
5, Ansari Road
Daryaganj, New Delhi-110002
Phone: 011-47034999, 9811692060
E-mail: books@gyanbooks.com

Distribution Network
gyanbooks.com
India, USA, Canada, UK, Australia, France

ISBN : 978-81-212-6314-6 (PB)
First Published, 1879

2nd Impression 2022

Printed at: Gyan Press, Delhi.

THE SECRET OF A CLEAR HEAD
Author: J. MORTIMER GRANVILLE

THE SECRET

OF

A CLEAR HEAD.

BY

J. MORTIMER GRANVILLE.

Sixth Thousand.

1879.

TO THE READER.

THE following papers form the complement of those published some months back under the title of "COMMON MIND TROUBLES." The whole might have appeared in a single volume with the designation chosen for the present, but it seemed better to issue the two series separately. This I have done, and they follow not inaptly my "MINDS AND MOODS."

I can only repeat what I said in the preface to the last collection of papers: they were not written for professional readers; but for the generous reception accorded to them in quarters where I had no right to expect they would be, even, noticed I must express my obligation. I shall not be sorry if in examining the contents of this little book the reader adopts a practice familiar to the impatient devourer of fiction, and attacks the last chapter first.

When reviewers complain that I do not *prescribe* for my readers they pay me the best of compliments. The sole purpose I have set myself in these papers is to help the worried and weak to *avoid* the peril of mind disease. Medical men cannot, however much they may feel disposed to, impart to laymen that knowledge of disease without which it is an act of audacity to undertake the treatment of the simplest affection, and they are not, in my opinion, justified in addressing the unskilled community in works which, while they pretend to counsel, cannot fail to mislead. Meanwhile, I am not less strongly convinced that it is the bounden duty of every professor of physic to do all that lies in his power to promote the health of the people. It is his mission to preach the gospel of *health.* I am trying to do this, so far as I am able.

J. MORTIMER GRANVILLE.

April, 1879.

CONTENTS.

TEMPERATURE.

SUCH expressions as a "cool head," "hot-headed," and the like, commonly relate to temperament rather than temperature; but it is essential to a full comprehension of the subject before us that the *rationale* of animal heat should be stated, and the laws that govern the phenomenon of temperature actual and subjective, at least cursorily, explained.

Heat and the sensation of heat are two widely different states. When, on a chilly day or after washing in cold water, a man rubs his hands until a glow of heat seems to suffuse them, there is a very slight rise of actual temperature caused by the friction; the feeling is principally due to nerve-excitement, produced mechanically by the rubbing. The blood flows more freely into, and through, the parts excited immediately afterwards, as shown by the redness, but the first impression of heat is mainly one of sensation. The feeling and the fact are not even constantly related. A person may feel hot when not only the surrounding temperature but that of his body is low ; or, he may feel cold when really over-heated. These perverted sensations are occasionally morbid—that is to say, form part of a state of disease—or they may arise from individual peculiarities which, perhaps, render perceptions of a particular class especially acute. On the other hand, there are conditions of the body, and special sensibilities, in which the sense of heat is dulled, and even considerable elevations of temperature are not perceived. It is easy to see how impossible it must be to form a correct judgment of the actual state of heat either around or within us by simple sensation.

The animal body makes its own heat, and is so far independent that, if it can be protected from the cooling or heating influences of the outer world, it will maintain an equal and healthful temperature. The source of heat is food, which in the subtle processes of the living organism acts as fuel and undergoes oxidation or "combustion." In the absence of sufficient or suitable food, or—what is the same thing in effect—when, from any cause, the normal functions of digestion and assimilation are impaired, the body is not properly heated from within, and the subject feels cold. A great deal has been written about the most suitable food for heat-producing purposes. No doubt it is true that substances in which the fatty elements preponderate have a special tendency to generate heat, but in experience and fact, food that nourishes the body also warms it.

The heating process is not, as was once supposed, worked out by any special organ. Neither the lungs nor the liver form the focus of combustion ; the work is done in detail all over the body, and not in a special centre. The blood that courses through the vessels is not merely a "heat-carrier" but a heat-producer. It holds in solution the elements of food taken up from the digestive organs, prepared for use, and destined to serve as material, to supply the demand created by the consumption of tissue in the vital functions of the body. Each tissue selects from the blood brought into contact with it, by the wondrous network of capillary vessels, the particular elements it requires. In a rough sort of way, this process of nutrition may be illustrated by saying that it is carried on much as the process of growth in a plant is performed by the selective and appropriative power of the rootlets which strike into the soil, or, in the case of water-plants, lie submerged in the fluid ; what is needed is absorbed and assimilated, the rest is allowed to pass. In the course of this chemico-vital proceeding new combinations of material take place and heat is generated.

If the quantity of material appropriated is in excess of the systemic requirements or the nutrition of any part of the body is carried on too hurriedly —perhaps because it has been previously exhausted by over-work, or starved—an excess of heat may be set up either throughout the body as a whole, in which case there is fever, or in a part of the organism, producing what is called inflammation. Disturbance of nutrition, destroying the relations of health, whether caused by "chill," mechanical injury, or poison, either organic or inorganic, may cause a condition of disease to be established, but when that exists, however caused, the phenomenon of increased temperature is the immediate effect of disorderly nutrition. When from any cause nutrition fails, or is defective, an opposite, but not less abnormal state—deficiency of heat—results; the chemico-vital processes are not carried on in their integrity, and the temperature of the body is lowered, as in starvation.

Throughout the world, whether man be placed in tropical heat or arctic cold, the temperature of his body must, to maintain health, be preserved at the same point—about 98·4 to ·6 degrees of Fahrenheit. A very small departure from this universal mean standard constitutes or indicates disease. The external heat is comparatively unimportant, or only of secondary moment, in the economy of nature; we cannot rely upon it for the compensation of differences in the heat generated within the body by the organism. Except for the production of a temporary effect, such as to give time for the re-establishment of the normal temperature in a body chilled, as by submersion, external heat is useless for vital purposes. The only way in which it can act is by preventing the loss of more heat, and giving a slight aid to recovery by warming the surface of the body.

If when a person is cold he goes into a heated apartment, or sits before a large fire, he receives with advantage just as much heat as will bring the skin of his body up to the normal standard; as soon as that point is reached, the organism will begin to labour to get rid of the superfluous caloric, and by sweating the heat must be kept from rising above the standard. All the heat thrust upon the body above 98·6 degs. is waste and mischievous except in so far as it may promote perspiration, which probably helps to work off some of the useless and burdensome, possibly morbid and poisonous, materials that oppress the system. This is how Turkish baths, and "sweatings" generally, do good, by exciting increased activity of the skin, and as it were, opening up new ways of egress for matters which, if retained, might offend.

So far as the heat of the body is concerned, whether in health or disease, every degree of external heat which is above the complement to form 98·6 degs. Fahr. with the heat of the body itself at the time, is useless and may do harm. It follows that in fever the surrounding atmosphere should be kept cool; in depressing disease, when the heat-producing powers of the organism are small, the air around should be warm. These are precisely the conclusions to which experience and observation conduct us; and the facts now briefly stated explain the reason why.

There is no warmth in clothes; the heat comes from the body itself, generated within, or the surrounding atmosphere, or from substances with which the body may be in contact. Of course clothes, like any other materials, can be charged with heat, and will take up as much thermic or heating property as their specific capacity allows. It is this capability of receiving heat which constitutes the first condition of warmth in the comparative value of different materials of dress. The second condition consists in the physical power of any fabric to hold the heat with which the article has been charged. For example, some materials will became warmer in a given time and retain their heat longer than others under the same conditions of exposure, first to heating and then to cooling influences. The principle of clothing should be to protect the body from external conditions which tend to abstract heat, when the surrounding temperature is lower than that of the body; and to strike heat into the organism, when the temperature of the outside air and of the substances with which the skin may be brought into contact is higher than that of the animal body itself.

The *absorption* of heat is determined by the degree in which the body is colder than the surrounding temperature. As we have said, no more external heat is wanted by the organism than will suffice to bring it up to 98·4 or 6° Fahr., and even this aid may readily be dispensed with if there be no abstraction or loss of heat from within. Practically therefore we do not need to absorb heat, and, in a temperate though changeful climate, are more deeply interested in keeping the heat we make in winter, and defending ourselves from the access of heat from without in summer by moderate measures, than in devising precautions against either extreme. Nature attaches more importance to internal heat that to variations of external temperature. She has given the inhabitants of the Torrid Zone dark skins because these are better for the radiation of heat than white, although the dark colour absorbs more rapidly than the lighter. On the other hand, she has given the denizen of the Frigid Zone a pale skin, and clothed the Polar bear with a white fur because white does not so freely part with the heat it holds or covers, as black.

Radiation of heat takes place when the surroundings are cool, and, if the radiating body be a living animal organism, the aim must be to prevent too rapid dispersion. This points to the choice of materials and colours for clothing which hold the heat in winter, and of those which, so to say, resist it in summer. *Reflection* is in practice a part of radiation, except that the reflecting body may, in theory at least, be impervious to the heat it throws off from its surface, while that which, more strictly speaking, radiates must first have become charged with caloric. *Evaporation* is the great cooling process by which perspiration reduces the temperature of the body. When Nature covers the body with fluid the physical effect intended is the same which we produce artificially by sprinkling the surface of any object with water. In the act of passing off as vapour, the fluid takes away heat and thus cools the skin.

This is, in some measure, how sweating reduces the heat of the body in fever, and, in the absence of a continuous cause of mischief or when the poison has done its baneful work and become exhausted, gives relief. The ancients used to think more of "critical sweatings" than modern physicians do; but it cannot be doubted that when a disease —of which excessive heat-production is a feature— runs its course naturally, copious perspiration commonly occurs at the crisis, and the evaporation that follows helps to reduce the temperature. There are of course other natural methods by which the heat of the body may be reduced. For example, discharges of all kinds will carry off heat; but those from within generally take place when some large internal organ has been the seat of an accumulation of heating material which the system has been unable to take up. For slighter ailments of the febrile order, surface-evaporation is generally preferred by Nature, and is commonly found to suffice.

Local temperature, that is, the heat in the several regions of the body is determined by conditions which control the circulation of the blood, and the function of nutrition or food appropriation. If the circulation is free in a part, its temperature is maintained; if, from any cause, the flow of blood is retarded, the local heat will be reduced. Any one may put this to the test by encasing the hands in somewhat tight gloves when the weather is cold. The pressure prevents the free passage of the blood through the vessels, and the temperature falls. There is no warmth of any kind in the gloves; they act simply as non-conductors of heat, and prevent the heat generated within the body from passing off. For example—if a piece of lint or rag be dipped in cold water and laid on the skin, and a sheet of impervious or non-conducting material, such as india-rubber or thick flannel, is wrapped closely round, the heat of the body will raise the cold water to a temperature at which it will be given off as steam the moment the covering is removed. When the extremities are enclosed in thick or dense coverings, their temperature will depend on the amount of heat generated within them, and if the flow of blood through the vessels is arrested or retarded, nothing is gained, but everything lost, by the measures taken to protect them from the external cold.

This is a matter of the highest practical moment, and needs to be thoroughly understood. The feet cannot be kept warm unless the blood circulates freely in the extremities, and that will not be the case if the boot, shoes, or stockings are tight. These last-named articles of clothing are practically the worst offenders. A stocking encircling the foot and leg closely and enveloping every part, with special pressure at the instep, around the ankle. and above or below the knees, must inevitably tend to oppose the circulation and so reduce the natural heat. The arteries which bring the blood to the extremity are set deeper than the veins that carry it back, and, as the latter are provided with valves which open towards the heart, it is too commonly supposed that the "support" afforded by the stocking will favour the return of blood more than it can impede the deeper supply-currents, and so help the circulation; but practically we know this is not the fact, for a tight stocking ensures a cold foot, and the chilliness of which many persons complain is mainly caused by the practice of gartering, and wearing stockings which constrict somewhere or everywhere.

There is a popular notion that if the feet are cold the head must be hot, and by keeping the extremities warm with wraps the "blood is drawn from the head," and its temperature reduced. Those who have on the one hand studied the phenomenon of fever, and on the other noted the physical condition of races and individuals who habitually leave the extremities unclothed, will know that this theory of the distribution of heat is only partially true. Heat depends on the due supply of nutrient elements to the tissues. It is the expression or result of the process of local feeding. If a part is active it will be heated. When the feet are left bare the complex muscular apparatus of the extremity, which in a stiff shoe scarcely works, is called into vigorous action, the arch of the foot plays with every step, and each toe performs its share in the act of progression. This promotes growth and calls for nutrition, whereby the heat is maintained; whereas if it be simply packed away as a useless piece of organism, no amount of external heat will warm it. Work is the cause and counterpart of heat throughout the body.

The same principle applies to the head. No amount of external cooling will reduce the temperature, no drawing away of the blood by artificial expedients will permanently relieve the sense or obviate the fact of heat if the organ within the cranium is excessively or morbidly active. The brain is a peculiarly delicate and complicated organ, requiring more prompt and constant nutrition than any other part of the body, because the constituent elements of its tissue change more rapidly than those of any other in proportion to the amount of exercise. Moreover, the brain is always acting during consciousness, and even in sleep it is seldom wholly at rest, as we know from the occurrence of dreams. The faculty of nutrition is highly developed in the organ or it could not so continuously, and ont he whole healthily, discharge its functions, even when other parts of the body, or the system as a whole, are suffering from disease. When the head is heated there is nearly always a local cause for it, and the remedy must be addressed to the seat of the malady. The temporary expedient of "drawing away the blood" by applying heat to the extremities is useful as far as it goes, and may suffice to enable the organ to rid itself by the contraction of its blood-vessels from a surplus charge of this fluid, but in the absence of special causes the *reason* of the "heat of head" is undue exercise or disturbance of nutrition in the brain itself. Perhaps the seat of the over-work and consequent heating may have been limited to a particular part of the head; for example, the apparatus of sight, or hearing, as when the head becomes heated by reading too long or in a strong light. The point to understand is that when the head is physically hot it is the seat of too much or disorderly nutrition, and either the amount of brain or sense-power exercised must be reduced or the mode of action changed, and the particular part of the apparatus of perception or thought which has been too severely taxed relieved.

From these general observations—recapitulating a few only of the more notable facts in relation to heat and heat production—we may draw the following conclusions. First, the heat of the body depends on its own condition and functions rather than on the temperature of the objects by which it is surrounded. There is a wonderful power of self-preservation and adaptation to external needs provided in the constitution of man, and his chief aim should be to aid instead of hindering the exercise of this beneficent faculty. Second, external temperature ought to be treated rather as an enemy than a friend; and the body should be so trained as to resist its variations. If we rely on the aid of the heat without to help the heat within, we must expect to be chilly when the weather is cold, and responsive to all its variations. The body which seems out of health in cold weather is essentially unhealthy: it is deficient in the power of heat-generation, and unless it can be shown that some accidental waste is going on which depresses the vital powers, and so accounts for this weakness of function, it may be assumed that either the heart is feeble or diseased, the blood-vessels are out of condition, or there is a defect somewhere in the apparatus of nutrition. The true condition of health is that in which the temperature of the body as a whole and of its several parts is not disturbed by surroundings either of heat or cold. Third, the preservation of a natural and healthy temperature is mainly to be secured by the maintenance of a regular and well distributed circulation of blood charged with the materials of nutrition.

The first condition of a free and continuous flow of blood is a healthy heart, not hampered by irritants, mental or physical. Sudden grief or fright produces cold by arresting the circulation, and the flow may be permanently retarded by anxiety. The mind has a wondrously direct influence on the heart and blood-vessels—on the latter through the nerves, which increase or reduce the calibre of the minute arteries, as in blushing or blanching at a thought. Instead of loading the body with clothes, the "chilly" should search out the physical cause of their coldness. The blood must not only circulate freely; it must be rich in nourishing materials, and not charged with poison. An excess of any one element may destroy the value of the whole. It is too much the habit of valetudinarians and unhealthy people of all kinds, to charge the blood with substances supposed to be "heating" or "cooling" as they think the system requires them. This is a mistake. The body does not need to be pampered with cordials, or refrigerated with cunningly devised potions. If it is well nourished it will be healthy.

—:o:—

HABIT.

It is surprising to find, on close scrutiny, how large a proportion of the acts we perform, seemingly at the bidding and under the control of the will, are in truth performed unconsciously. Walking, running, leaping, lifting and carrying burdens—in fact, most of the actions in which the muscular system i engaged—are accomplished without the cognisance of details. The end only is perceived; the will is engrossed with the result, and ignores the steps by which it is reached. We set out to walk on a particular road to a certain place; the feet and legs are set in motion and we continue walking, while the whole attention is absorbed with matters of thought, no concern being bestowed on the management of the limbs unless unusual or unexpected sensations attract the notice of the mind. We carry a book or a parcel, and hold it, though its possession may be forgotten. In short, there is a power of setting a part of the organism to do certain work and leaving the task to be carried out by a subordinate faculty of superintendence, which discharges its function unconsciously.

Take as an illustration one of the commonest actions performed by most of us once or twice daily —that of lifting the water-jug from a washing-stand. We will to pour out some water, and expect to find it in the jug. The muscular movements requisite for grasping the handle of the vessel and raising it are performed automatically, and the proper amount of force is put out to raise the weight of water we are accustomed to find. It happens that the servant has neglected to fill the jug, and up it goes with a bound. Again, we are walking up stairs, habit leads us to expect another step at the top; the leg is raised, and comes down with a jerk because the anticipated stair is not there to receive the foot; or perhaps we are coming down, and the foot is arrested by the level floor when we expected a further descent. These are common experiences, but they possess a high significance, and may stand for typical examples of a large group of actions which are performed unconsciously. The sort of unconsciousness which characterises these acts is made evident by the nature of the misadventures which have been instanced.

When anything is done for the first time, it requires to be worked out by the will, each step of the performance is intentional; as when a child learns to walk, or a pianoforte player to strike the proper notes with the right fingers in the due relations of time by appropriate muscular movements of hand and wrist. When once the combination of acts is mastered, the will no longer superintends the exercise. The attention is not only withdrawn, but it *must* be diverted, or, in other words, the performance left to the supervision of the subordinate faculty. Let any one who doubts this try to execute in detail, under the superintendence of the will, movements which are perfectly well done without consciousness; for example, to descend a flight of stairs rather rapidly, particularly noticing the planting of each foot on the step below, or to strike a few chords of music with conscious control of the several fingers employed. The unwonted attention embarrasses the performance, and in certain cases even renders it impossible. The explanation of this experience is that the will is wont to relegate the control of muscular movements which are habitually performed to the guidance of a sense which, while it cannot originate, is able to repeat combinations of movements to which it has been accustomed; and, having thus, so to say, delegated a portion of its authority—as the employer of a large number of workers entrusts the management of details to some confidential agent—the will ceases to trouble itself with these lesser matters, and they pass out of the sphere of consciousness.

In certain morbid states this delegation is impossible, and the muscular system will do nothing it is not directly willed to perform. Physiologists and pathologists cite the case of a nurse who could not hold a child in her arms unless she kept it constantly in mind. The moment her attention was diverted from the business in hand her arms dropped, and she let the infant fall. This instance will suffice to illustrate the principle. The conclusion is, briefly, that much that we do is done unconsciously—the actions which fall into this class are, for the most part, matters of habit; and, in proportion as things come to be subjects of habit, they are likely to be done unconsciously.

What is habit? The apologist for humanity in its least noble phase asserts that "habit is second nature." It would be more explicit to say that habit is memory supplemented by an unconscious reasoning on the simple lines of a direct inference from the known to the unknown. I use the phrase "unconscious reasoning" advisedly. There are more than sufficient grounds for believing that a certain sort of reasoning may proceed without an appeal to the judgment, and without the cognisance of the higher intellect—in short, without consciousness. While the mind is engrossed with one subject, the lesser faculties may be actively employed with another, and even work out processes which, when they come to be reviewed, appear complex. By this reasoning the sleep-walker adapts his proceedings to the requirements of the surrounding circumstances, his brain being all the while asleep and he in a state of unconsciousness. This sort of reasoning probably differs in no essential particular from the phenomenon of "instinct" with which the animals below man in the scale of intelligence are gifted, and which sometimes seems in its exercise to emulate the power of reflection and judgment.

An unconscious expectancy that circumstances and events will shape themselves on the pattern of some previous experience would appear to be the dominant principle of habit. Such an expectancy governs the conduct and determines the amount and kind of energy put forth. In the instance of the water-jug, the force brought to bear on the vessel is that which has been found by experience to be appropriate for lifting the expected weight. There is no conscious thought about the matter ;

but the lesser faculty of reasoning—call it instinct or what we may—argues from the past to the future.

The proof that there is something more than memory at work, and that a process of reasoning takes place, may be found in the fact that while an empty jug is raised with a jerk, a small jug is never lifted as though it were a large one by too much force being applied, although the jug that is raised may be smaller than the one we are accustomed to lift. The eye informs the lesser faculty, and the force put out is just enough to raise the full jug. It is only when the jug is empty that the jerk occurs. In both cases, however—when the jug is smaller than usual as well as when it is empty—the act of lifting is performed without thought, that is unconsciously. Another illustration will make this clearer. When a man is walking along the road engrossed in thought he may trip in a shadow. His attention is not directed to the appearance until after the act of stumbling ; but, before that took place, the shadow across his path had cheated the lesser faculty of instinct, and induced the performance of exceptional movements, which, not being really necessary, caused the fault.

Habit in regard to the muscular system is a repetition of acts previously performed, and ranging from grotesque and meaningless contortions or grimaces to the unconscious performance of well ordered and even elaborately conceived and intentional processes—that is, processes intended to produce a certain result, and so employed—as when the worker proceeds with his task, and even performs complex modifications and combinations of processes while his thoughts are far away, and the product of his skill afterwards impresses his aroused attention with surprise. For example, the turner with lathe and gouge, forgetful of his task, produces a ball, and turns it well, but instead of a socket! He was thinking of something else, and laboured on by habit. Habit in regard to the mind is of the same nature, and exposed to the like vagaries. For example, the accountant, with mind busy on some topic of greater interest than that before him, adds instead of subtracting, or multiplies in place of dividing; and what he does is well done, though not the thing he intended to do. "His mind was wandering." It had, in fact, strayed far away from the scene and subject of his task, which was performed by a lesser faculty, perfectly well able to work out a process of reasoning based on experience but not capable of originating the appropriate motive idea which the end in view required.

It would save a world of trouble, and lead to the correction of a multitude of misconceptions, if this sort of blunder could be understood, and the errors of unconscious reasoning eliminated. Unfortunately the difficulty of bringing the facts plainly before the mind, and making it conscious of its own unconsciousness, is very great. The intellect will not admit that it is ever caught napping, and it is unaware that a large part of its functions are discharged by deputy. Nineteen persons out of twenty will, for example, be scandalised to hear that they do not even spell consciously, although this fact is brought home to them daily by the circumstance that in order to be quite sure how to spell many a word, they find it necessary to write it. The act of writing a word is performed automatically, like playing a chord in music, and it is only by going through the process under the control of instinct, by "habit" instead of thought, and looking at the result, that they can attain the certainty intentional judgment will not supply.

A further proof of the truth of this hypothesis will be furnished by the experiment of trying to spell the word in writing with some unaccustomed instrument—for example, a type-writing machine, or telegraph apparatus. Persons who have been accounted good etymologists and practised spellers find, when they come to strike the alphabet keys in rapid succession to spell a word, that they are often at fault in the commonest combination. This experience is not universal, but it is widespread and significant. The spelling of words has come to be performed unconsciously, and when the will is required to resume the duty it has delegated to the subordinate faculty, it is found to be incompetent for its discharge without training afresh.

As with the arrangement of letters in words, so is it with the composition of words to form sentences. Those who have formed the "habit" of speaking extemporaneously can seldom compose in writing with equal facility, and the converse. Authors and orators are prone to repeat themselves; and men who have gone on writing or speaking for many years have, in fact, stored their mind with phrases which instinct employs with a rapidity and method that does duty for thought: so that, given a subject, writers and speakers alike string sentences together with scarcely any exercise of the higher intellectual faculties, and can almost write in their sleep.

Instances have been known, authenticated beyond question, in which writers have composed articles, coherent and even well-written, while in a state bordering on mental unconsciousness, and certainly with the minimum of mind-action on the work performed. This duality of the mental powers doubtless differs greatly in individuals. Some can accomplish little or nothing without a direct and conscious effort of the will, while others can do almost anything they are in the habit of doing without conscious endeavour. To be "a practised hand" at anything, and to have acquired by long and frequent exercise a special facility for performing any act, whether physical or mental, is, in short, to have delegated the performance to the faculty of instinct, or lesser intelligence below the will; and it is always a scientific, and in most cases a practical, possibility that what is so done may, under special circumstances, be done unconsciously.

This last remark carries us straight to the conclusion towards which we have been working. Unconscious energy, or habit controlled by instinct, will produce results the most astounding, and account for the strangest of so-called spiritualistic or somnambulistic "manifestations." It is not only unnecessary, but unscientific, to assume that the perpetrators of many seeming "impostures"—using that term with regard to the nature of the performance rather than its intention—practise conscious deception. Take the case of a so-called "medium." It is by no means certain that the act of "spirit writing" or "trance talking" is an intentional fraud. It is comparatively easy to form any habit, and one of speaking or writing without thinking is readily attainable.

The process by which this exploit is performed is that which I have attempted to describe—a delegation of control to the subordinate faculty, so that it may go on without thought, and at length without consciousness. When such a habit is formed it is obviously practicable for the individual himself, or some other person, to distract or displace his attention—even to send his mind to sleep—while the lower faculty remains awake and performs simple processes of reasoning, displaying sagacity, and to a certain extent employing or superseding the senses. This is the condition of the somnambulist, and it is one which may, in special cases, be induced at pleasure by the will of the subject or another. What are called mesmeric passes, or any other mode of signifying the wish or diverting the mind, may be employed, and, the consciousness being taken off, the lower intelligence the latter will be left free to work.

The scope of the instinctive or lesser faculty is, as we have seen, limited to recollection, or the simpler forms of reasoning by inference; but by development in practice this lesser intelligence is doubtless susceptible of improvement and a seeming extension of capacity. The process by which mediums and mesmeric subjects with somnambulistic capablities can be trained may be gathered from what sometimes happens in the case of persons addicted to talking in their sleep. It is not unfrequently possible to engage the sleep-talker, and, by judiciously asking questions, to carry on a conversation without awakening him. The result is the same, though the process is reversed, when the medium or somnambulist is sent to sleep while his lesser faculty of reasoning is engaged in the business of a *séance*.

A morbid or weak state of mind facilitates the production of the state described, and each exercise renders the diversion of consciousness and sleep-production more easy. The point on which I would insist is that the actor is really unconscious, and possibly believes he is the subject of supernatural influences. The same is true of the table-turner. He is unconscious of the physical force he exerts on the article of furniture; and those who act with him, when once the movement begins, are thrown into the same state, and unconsciously contribute their share of energy to the production of the result. Unconscious mind-action and muscular movement are, in truth, very common; and these phenomena abundantly explain the otherwise startling and inexplicable effects ignorantly ascribed to influences which, so far as we are aware, have no existence.

The moral—or rather the common-sense inference—to be drawn from these considerations is the warning that it is unwise and imprudent, in the interests of a clear head, to push the habit of doing things unconsciously beyond legitimate limits. People are, as a rule, very apt to be proud of the character of experts, and take great credit for the attainment of automatic dexterity. The pianist who can execute the most complicated movements without a false fingering is proud of his achievement, although he may have little or no real taste for music. The author who can produce several works simultaneously, and turn out three-volume novels with the greatest celerity, is congratulated on his capacity, although half the work he does is, in fact, mechanical.

The world judges by results, and takes little account of ways of working and processes. Thought is scarcely appreciated as an ingredient of literary or artistic work. Whether the product comes from the intellect or the instinct, whether it has been evolved by mental labour or produced in great part unconsciously, is a matter of profound indifference to the assessor of value, who deals only with what is done, and disregards the doing. Meanwhile, those who have health and vigour of mind in view will be prudent to bestow intentional thought on what they do rather than rely on the lesser faculty too extensively.

A very large proportion of the energy put out by man must be placed at the disposal of the lower intelligence, but the less the mind is allowed to wander from the business in hand, and the more constantly it is content to do one thing at a time, and that thoroughly, the less will the mind and body be left at the mercy of "habit," the more will habit be under control of the will, and the less danger can there be of that development of the duality of the intellect, and alienation of the higher reasoning faculty and consciousness from the animal instinct, which is so apt to culminate in disease, and to render the subject beside himself—a disorganised brain-worker, a monomaniac.

—:o:—

TIME.

Nature sets the example of measuring time by days, months, and seasons; we only work out the division and subdivision by telling off in hours the period which composes a day and night, and counting the four seasons as a year. The method of time-keeping we adopt is arbitrary, though more exact, so far as the experience of time is concerned, than that of the great mistress; but it is under her guidance and at her suggestion we have recourse to the expedient of marking the passage of time, which otherwise would speed unheeded in its monotonous progress. The investigations of science would be impossible without a system of time-measurement, the operations of mind would be wild exercises and indefinite, and life itself must sink to the level of bare existence, without hope of the future, interest in the present, or accurate recollection of the past. If the reckoning of time were lost, and with it the power of instituting a new record, life at home would be difficult, exploration impossible, chaos would resume the place of order, and so far as man was concerned, the world must fall back into the state described as "without form and void."

Measuring time is a faculty developed by instinct, though perfected and applied by knowledge. It exists in every savage race; even those tribes which lack the power of counting above very limited numbers have that of noting the lapse, and in some way estimating the progress, of time. It is not however with what may perhaps be called the natural history of this subject, or even its scientific aspect, that we are at the moment concerned. There is a great mental and moral phase of the subject of time-measuring, to which attention may be usefully directed.

First, let us jot down a few of the common but curious experiences which most of us have in some form encountered in the measuring of time. How different is the seeming rate of progress under divers conditions and amid dissimilar circumstances, or to opposite temperaments under the like conditions and with the same surroundings, or to the same individual mind in various moods! These differences are so well recognised that it is not worth while to dwell upon them. It must not be forgotten that the expression "progress of time" is purely metaphorical, and the discrepancy between the estimates formed of the ceaseless advance, by independent observers and under diverse conditions, shows the imperative need of a common measure by which to compare experiences. Meanwhile it is interesting and useful to seek the cause of these discrepancies.

Searching to the root of the matter, it would seem to be this. Time is like a chain—if we tell it off link by link, it seems longer than if we only glide along it to the end. If the thought possesses us that every link is an obstacle or a stage which has to be passed before we can reach the extremity the progress seems slow; while, on the other hand, if each link is looked upon as a step bringing us nearer the goal, the seeming passage is marked with great celerity. The mind generally takes its tone from the nature of the end in view. If that be longed for, the process of link-counting is wearisome, and seems slow ; if the end is dreaded, successive links slip through the fingers with lightning speed.

This is a general statement of the rule, and therefore not without many apparent exceptions. For example, no one loves pain; nevertheless the time which passes immediately before the performance of an expected operation seems wondrously tardy. The reason is that the object on which the mind has fixed its attention is not the suffering that is to be endured, but the point beyond, when ease will be procured, or the ordeal will be over. This explains the difference of feeling with which the approach of death is regarded by persons with and without hope of the future. If there be a joyous anticipation of coming happiness, the thoughts are fixed on the bright future beyond, and the act of death becomes the last stage of a journey it is earnestly desired to complete. If there be no hope, or, from any cause, death assumes the aspect of a penalty or overwhelming disaster, it is the object of dread, and the time that ushers it in passes too rapidly.

The precise mental process by which the passage of time is made to seem slow or fast may be described as one of concentration. If the attention be directed to details, and each little incident of the way becomes the subject of special cognisance, time moves slowly; whereas, if the end only is thought of, and the episodes of the interval are counted as hindrances, they seem to block the way and defer the realisation of hope interminably. Another notable experience, the converse of that last described, is the difference between time past and time future—looking back and looking forward. The explanation of this difference will be found in the facts already stated. It is because the mind, when glancing behind, loses sight of the daily procession of events, that the time past seems short; whereas the future is full of plans and purposes which attract the mind to the path, and give the sense of distance. If some particular object of hope—as the attainment of man's estate and fancied freedom to a youth—rivets the attention and diverts it from the road by which it will have to be reached, then the desired object seems near. The impression is in each case directly dependent on the manner in which the mind views the object, and the experience is wholly subjective.

It may appear idle to speak of the present, for while we think of it the fleeting moment passes. Nevertheless, there are states of feeling in which time drags like a galling chain over the bruised body, and others when the spirit bounds forward so joyously that it takes no thought of time, and the winged hours pass unheeded. These opposite sensations are determined by the conditions explained previously, and depend on the feelings with which the mind looks around or forward, and back on the past, with the consciousness of being hurried on or retarded in its progress. In this sense there *is* a mental and physical cognisance of the passing instant of time, and there is a *present*. Now let us try to see what these slight and suggestive, rather than elucidatory, considerations are worth in the practical bearings of the mind and consciousness towards life in its diverse forms and moods, its grateful and untoward experiences.

To make time go slowly, or seem long when we look back upon it, it must be well filled with incidents which engross the attention and leave a record in legible marks on the memory. Few lives are wholly colourless or devoid of "experiences," but the least varied, if also they are objectless and uninspired by some engrossing purpose, are the longest to look forward upon, the briefest in retrospect. The future lies before the mental vision as a vista straight and immeasurable, because unmeasured; the trail behind is like a track across the desert, traceable only for a short distance, and seemingly short. By marking the way with white stones the path may be made a pleasant object to retrace in thought, and the more numerous these records the longer and better defined it will appear. Black and mournful remembrancers produce the same effect, and give the feeling of having lived long in the world; but, in the latter case, the feeling produced is one of weariness, while, in the other, a sense of maturity and "experience" may be enjoyed which inspires happiness and a consciousness of strength rather than discontent and exhaustion. In either event it is the busy life that seems the longest, whether the business in hand be good or bad, useful or mischievous.

The precept to be inferred from these premisses is so plain that it stands in little need of argument to enforce it. Those who would have the sense of happy maturity to cheer them in their later years, when the consciousness of waning energy begins, must live with a purpose and worthily while life is young and vigorous. Nothing so effectually prepares the mind for rest as the knowledge of having laboured to some good result. And those who can look back on the amplest tale of work accomplished enjoy the feeling of having lived the longest, and being ready to lay down the responsibility of life with the satisfaction of duty discharged and the least regret or disappointment in surrendering it. And so it is with the present and the future. If we would have time pass lightly, with none of that painful sense of being burdened or wearied, and having to resort to all sorts of devices to "pass time" and "kill time" which embitters the existence of many folk, there is nothing for it but to set the mind earnestly on some object towards which the energy may strive.

It is not enough to occupy the time; mere industry may, as we have seen, have the effect of making time go slowly by turning the incidents of daily duty into difficulties. This explains why a multitude of ease-seeking people find no relief or lightening of the burden of life in occupation. The task undertaken has no purpose. *It* alone engrosses the thoughts, and, instead of carrying time forward, it seems to clog and weary the spirit. This must always be the effect of work without a purpose. It sets the mind counting the hours before the task will be completed, and the soul wears out more rapidly, while the leaden foot of time does not seem to move any faster. When work or occupation gives energy and hope, when it lightens the darkness and brightens the daylight, it has a purpose. The mind does not count the enterprise a task without reward, but a means to some end on which the eye of faith and expectancy is fixed. Life, to be happy, must have an object and a future; nothing else can sweeten it or make it pass pleasantly and briskly.

It is well that milestones are set up by custom in this world of ours to mark how the years go by and offer each wayfarer a standard by which to measure his own progress. A host of personal questions crowd in on the mind with every occasion which reminds us that another period of time has passed away. Has the year, that is just concluded, gone with us more or less rapidly than those which have preceded it? The fact that the *details* of this recent page in our record are fresh in memory, while those which have gone before are perhaps forgotten, will tend to mislead the judgment and make the last period seem busier and better spent than its predecessors. Allowance must be made for this defect in the register kept by conscience. It is generally a bad sign when the recent past seems short and the near future long.

The spirit is weak, or there is not much to cherish fondly in the memory, no good pile of work to regard with pleasure, none of that legitimate pride that a sense of honourable industry inspires.

The estimate of time which each individual makes for himself is of high interest, and, if rightly judged by the common standard, may help to throw an instructive light on character. Men measure time very variously. The old and the young make widely diverse calculations of the length of the past and the future. The good and bad view it from opposite stand-points and under different aspects. It is a happy and hopeful experience when the years that are gone seem like ripe sheaves of grain well garnered, the future looks all too short for the work to be accomplished, the happiness to be enjoyed, and a prize glitters in the distance to be worthily won in steadfast faith by loyal service.

The priceless virtue of patience shows itself in a wise and self-possessed method of measuring time, and the sorrow and pain of impatience are occasioned by inability to perform this natural and half-unconscious function in a spirit of intelligent respect for the laws that govern the procession of causes and effects. To cultivate that most excellent uality, the power of "waiting," on which success in life generally depends, should be one of the prominent aims of education, and, of course, of self-improvement. True patience is not so much the stern repression of a longing desire as the faculty of devoting due attention to means and processes without losing sight of the end. The object to be gained is kept steadily before the mind, but the intellect busies itself with the measures by which the desired result is to be attained.

Instead of lying down in feeble expectancy, the wise man works while he waits, and the enterprise in which he engages is in some way made contributory to the purpose by which he is animated. He is not indifferent to the progress of time or insensible of its tardy advance; but he shortens the seeming delay by filling, with acts of useful purpose, tending to the end in view and occupying the mind without exhausting it, the interval which must elapse before the fruition of his hopes. Patience is an active rather than a passive quality. It inspires with new energy, instead of wasting that which it exerts. The notion of sitting still while waiting is the cause of many a disastrous failure. The really patient are busy, and, in place of consuming strength, they devote it to progress, advancing the realisation of their desires and making the way seem less long by embellishing it with good and worthy exploits, which engross thought and save the mind from the blighting effects of disappointment and weariness.

None of us can avoid the daily practice of time-measuring. Those who affect to take no heed of time are either worried by the slow progress it seems to make or apt to be taken unawares by the discovery of the speed with which it flies from them. The only way to live peaceably and contentedly, free from boredom on the one hand or surprises on the other, is to make the method of time-measuring a subject of intelligent thought. The man who systematically sets himself to disregard the state of his worldly affairs deserves to be overtaken by misfortune. He can have no reasonable ground of complaint if things go ill with him. The bargain he makes with conscience is one in which he is to purchase the present ease of ignorance at the cost of ceaseless risk and final discomfiture. The man who essays to ignore the flight of time can seldom make even as good terms as these with Destiny. He pays the penalty of indifference in a present sense of heaviness and weariness nothing can compensate, and which only purpose and industry could relieve. His heart is not at ease when alone within its secret chambers His head is seldom, if ever, clear.

PLEASURE.

THE aphorism that no man can do well unless he takes pleasure in what he is doing is especially true of the varied forms of head-work, of every exercise in which the mind is primarily engaged. Meanwhile, not only do tastes differ widely with respect to the sources of personal happiness, but the strangest differences prevail as to the conditions under which individuals experience enjoyment. Some derive pleasure from the slightest causes of contentment, and are able to convert even adverse circumstances into occasions of rejoicing. Others need to be lifted, as it were, out of their accustomed surroundings, and to be inspired with some new spirit before they can be said to enjoy life or participate in the sense of genuine happiness.

The same object or occasion of pleasure will influence in totally diverse ways different persons equally moved by it. One will be stirred to enthusiastic delight by its contemplation, another will be thrown into a train of reflections awakening sentiments the most genial but not communicable to those around, while a third may seem scarcely affected, but nevertheless experience an inner sense of enjoyment, none the less real because set in a minor key and exclusively personal. These differences, and the infinite variety of manifestations in which they are displayed, illustrate the diversity of the sense of pleasure or happiness, an experience as variable in nature as in degree.

Pleasure is a state, and depends on the constitution and temper of the person by whom it is felt rather than the object or circumstance by which the feeling may be excited. The source or occasion of pleasure which moved us powerfully at one period of life, or in a certain mood, has no influence, or may even provoke disgust and melancholy, under different conditions of time, place, and temperament. Not only are several persons variously affected, the same individual may be inspired with totally diverse emotions by a scene, a story, an entertainment, or any object of taste, submitted as a means of gratification or happiness at different periods.

The faculty of enjoyment is personal, just as the power of producing a particular sound is located in a musical instrument. A skilful player will elicit better tones from a finely constituted and perfect instrument than can be produced from one which is defective, and, as there are performers able to extract melodious sounds from seemingly impracticable sources, so, under certain conditions, the least happy may be stirred to something like enjoyment; but the power, the sense, the capacity, of receiving agreeable impressions and enjoying the experience of pleasure, is part of the nature of man, and, like every other faculty, is dependent for its degree of acuteness on the development it has received in the course of training by accidental circumstances or design and education. It is the fashion to think and speak of the means of happiness as potent charms by which the instinct or sensibility must needs be affected; and, if a response is not elicited, the individual who fails to be amused, or give tokens of enjoyment, is pitied or condemned for his lack of sensibility, whereas perhaps his nature is keenly alive to impressions of pleasure, although the particular stimulant applied happens to be uncongenial.

The extent to which temper of mind and habits of thought influence the faculty of enjoyment, determining its susceptibility, and giving it a bias for or against special forms of excitement, is not sufficiently recognised. For example, a severely realistic view of life and its responsibilities may extinguish the power of deriving pleasure from works of fiction and imaginative entertainments, although the sense of pleasure may remain keenly alive to impressions of wit and humour which do not mock the manners and circumstances of society. Without the explanation this reflection supplies it seems strange to find men of sense, who are daily engrossed with oppressively gloomy and repulsive views of life and humanity, moved to merriment by trivial pleasantries and apparently susceptible of the most frivolous enjoyments, whereas the more intellectual entertainments which delight their inferiors in brain capacity have no power to please them.

The habit of stripping the tinsel from life, of penetrating the glamour which the conventionalities of society throw over existence, of analysing conduct and searching for motives, is so strong that it prevents the pleasure which others derive from the contemplation of artificial delineations of character and fictitious scenes and episodes. The man of law is not gratified with a drama which violates the principles of personal conduct and legal procedure; the professional anatomist is offended instead of pleased with the picture or piece of statuary which transgresses the laws of form and proportion; and the physician can derive no enjoyment from the contemplation of varieties of figure and colour which he is accustomed to regard as the indications of disease. In the same way and from the same cause, as the observant generally grow more experienced they lose the power of tolerating the defects and errors of an unreal drama, and the stage loses its influence; while, as the years roll on, the varied scenes of life come to be associated with disagreeable experiences, and more of sorrow than joy is called up when they are re-presented.

The habit of reflection is thus a hindrance to commonplace enjoyments. The practice of looking into futurity may be even more ruthlessly destructive. What, for instance, can be less conducive to the pleasure popularly expected from a clever theatrical entertainment than the forecast of that inevitable moment when the poor players, having spent their brief hour on life's stage, must in truth shuffle off the mortal coil? Nothing perhaps more painfully dispels the illusion of paint and gaudy happiness than such a forecast occurring to the mind of the spectator, say, in the middle of a burlesque. The thought which strays in on the consciousness of an ordinary thinker as a strange reflection is the key-note of some minds, and persons so biased are incapacitated for the enjoyment of particular forms of amusement, although their susceptibility for the impressions of pleasure springing from other sources is not impaired.

The antithesis of this last temperament illustrates the force of habit, in giving especial zest to the enjoyment derivable from fictitious scenes and personifications. It is a subject of common remark that actors are peculiarly fond of theatres, thus presenting a marked contrast to the experience of other professions, the members of which commonly seek their diversion as far as possible from the scenes of their daily labour. The true solution of the enigma is probably to be found in the fact that by the habit of assuming characters, and living, as it were, in a world of supposititious sentiment, the faculty of enjoyment acquires a special susceptibility for pleasures derived through the imagination, and the unreal comes almost to replace the real. In actual life the experience is reversed, and the comedian appears a sad mortal, while the tragedian revels in humorous views of existence as constitutional temperament or the mood impels him.

Habit is not less influential in developing predilections for particular forms and modes of enjoyment than in determining the degree of impressibility. Children and young people, brought up in the midst of associations linking the sense of pleasure with special scenes and exercises, naturally find their enjoyment in these objects and occupations. Country fashions differ from those connected with the town or the sea, and persons trained exclusively amid one set of surroundings fail to understand the enthusiasm displayed by those who have been associated with another set. Nevertheless the faculty is the same, and perhaps as keen, in both cases, though developed with such specialty as to be insensible to impressions other than those for which it has been trained.

Pleasure is infinite in its variety, and there is probably no form of excitement which is not more or less frequently pressed into its service. This consideration, which is a simple statement of fact, obviously strikes at the root of the conceit of "self-mortification" and "self-denial." Man is so thoroughly selfish in his moral nature that it is a purely groundless assumption to suppose that he ever really denies his dominant inclination. If the impulse gratified by any act of human life were not, for the moment at least, the strongest, it would not triumph over all other desires.

The only possible way in which a man can be truthfully said to deny himself—that is, to deprive himself of the pleasure he most covets—is when by some pledge or act of volition he has *previously* put it out of his power to gratify a particular wish or inclination; and even in that case it was his pleasure to make this sacrifice when he made it, and therefore it was at the moment an exercise from which he extracted enjoyment, though at the cost of future pain. The cant of self-sacrifice is therefore inadmissible; the pleasure of giving up constitutes for a time a superior enjoyment to that of possession. The better part is chosen because it is felt to be better.

The pleasure of hope in the future surpasses the transient joy of present experience, or the comfort of escape from fear outweighs the value of a momentary enjoyment with the dread of some penalty to follow. Even the anticipation of happiness in the far future ministers to the sense of enjoyment in a way that gratifies self. It follows that, while it may seem impossible to derive enjoyment from some of the austerities and privations to which men and women doom themselves, the truth is, these ascetics do enjoy their self-imposed hardships, and the claim of special merit for the self-sacrifice performed rests on no more real foundation than the credulity of those who, because they do not themselves comprehend the pleasure enjoyed, are simple enough to believe in its non-existence.

The wise man may affirm the superiority of his more solid sources of pleasure, the far-sighted may extol the enduring quality of his enjoyment because other pleasures are deceptive and fleeting, but none can truthfully deny that they find enjoyment in the exercises or ways of life to which they devote themselves, for the simple reason that if they did not prefer they would not choose them. Some count the future of greater moment than the present; but in this view there is an enjoyment of conscious wisdom and forethought with which no pleasure of possession can vie.

It is well when the faculty of pleasure-taking is so trained that it most readily responds to true and worthy forms of gratification. The responsibility of those upon whom the cultivation of this capacity devolves is not easily overstated. There is a great art in the culture; it is not possible to succeed by cutting off every impure or untrustworthy source, and thereby limiting the means, of enjoyment. The untasted sources of pleasure will acquire an especial charm from the abstinence so enforced, and when the mind, sated with a few enjoyments, is free to slake its thirst at all, there is danger that the draught may be intoxicating, and even deadly from excess.

Parents and guardians are not wise who seek to ensure the future happiness of their children by a policy of rigid exclusiveness. The theatre comes to be regarded as an elysium if an occasional visit is prohibited. A mild course of theatre-going, taking pieces as they are produced—the good and the bad together—while the judgment is pliant and open to correction by wise counsel, would save many an impulsive youth from plunging headlong into dissipation. The same principle applies to all enjoyments not absolutely inadmissible. It is better to face the fact that they must be encountered, and to avoid giving them an unnatural and exaggerated fascination by restriction. As a matter of experience, the attractions of the playhouse are not overpowering if only they be regarded in their place; which is neither exalted nor permanent in the category of amusements.

The like is true of the score of so-called "vanities" to which the mind is inclined—not uncommonly by the clumsy measures taken to direct it to sources of happiness vastly superior, but not at first sight so alluring. It is a lamentable issue of evil associations, or sinister influence, when prurient tastes give the faculty of enjoyment a bias to radically bad courses. This is too often the case with those who after years of injudicious restraint find their way into the full blaze of the world at the stage of development in which all the susceptibilities are the most active and readily impressed by surrounding influences.

It is not difficult to detect the existence of a depraved taste or faculty of enjoyment prevalent among the masses of society in all its grades. The public amusements generally and the fashions and habits of the world supply incontrovertible proof of the essentially low tone of morals which forms the key-note of social enjoyment. It is vain to deplore this evil if we do nothing to remedy its defects and avert its consequences. There is abundant scope for the exercise of personal virtue in this field. Every one of us should, for self, and those with whom we are associated in life, strive to develop a capacity for enjoyments above the level set by sinister examples. There is always a tendency downwards, which needs to be constantly resisted. I am not sure that the effort made by education to enlighten the masses is likely also to purify their intellectual tastes or effect a genuine improvement in the quantity and quality of their brain-power. The worst faults of coarseness and vice are not uncommonly found associated with the highest intellectual attainments. Mere culture in the literary and scholastic sense will not suffice to ennoble or eliminate the seeds of evil. Meanwhile high and pure views of life are compatible with what is sometimes called "ignorance." The head may be cultured at the cost of the heart; but it is the latter we need most earnestly to purify and elevate.

SELF-IMPORTANCE.

Fussy faces, care-worn faces, supercilious and cold faces, with here and there benevolent faces beaming with goodwill and friendliness, spring from the sense of self-importance. What must be the feelings of the man who goes about with the consciousness that the fate of nations, in large measure, depends upon his intelligence, address, and patriotism? It matters little whether the consciousness be real or imaginary; the personal effects are the same—and it is with these we are at the moment mainly interested.

Man-and-woman-kind may be ranged, by the expression they wear on their countenances, in two principal classes—the Somebodies who lord it more or less graciously over their fellows, and the anybodies who meekly, or otherwise, submit to be ruled, patronised, or oppressed. Those who have the bearing of being thoroughly contented with their lot, whether high or low, form an almost insignificant minority, about whose way through life, with its tame enjoyments and mitigated sorrows, it is not worth while to waste words—albeit these last are the only truly happy folk in the world, and their inanely-joyous faces glow with the blissful ignorance of human nature's worst and most worrying regrets, disappointments, and annoyances.

To be Somebody in statecraft, diplomacy, military skill and prowess, literature, science, art, commerce, or even manual industry, probably inspires a comforting sense of superiority, but it must entail a multitude of anxieties. Setting aside the burden of responsibility which presses heavily on sensitive shoulders, there is the perpetual effort to maintain the position gained. Much flapping and fluttering of wings will be necessary to keep the place in mid-air "over the heads of the people." The up-gazing multitude is apt to follow the flight of the eagle and his imitators, whether hawk or lark, wondrous curiously; and the consciousness that one is so watched cannot be wholly inspiriting. It may even embitter triumph to know that success has not been gracefully achieved.

Again, to be Somebody must be to feel that reverence is due to the dignity; and, if homage is not yielded willingly, which cannot be always the fact, there is the ever-present sense of vigilance to see that the full meed of respect is rendered or enforced. Self-assertion may come easily to certain minds; but it must, certainly, form part of the character, or things are sure to go awry. This constitutes a serious drawback to the advantage of feeling self-important. In short, the consciousness of superiority is scarcely an unqualified boon, and those of us who are not so gifted may be thankful to be spared the penalty distinction entails. Meanwhile the lack of cause for the mingled pleasure and pain of boastfulness leaves us free to compassionate the sorrows and inconveniences of the Somebodies with whom we are brought into contact; and there is no sincerer gratification to the insignificant than to pick holes in the virtues, point out the defects, execrate the vices, and playfully pity the weaknesses, of the great, the prosperous, the pampered, and the blest.

Somebodies, real and pretended, abound. It is difficult to move a step without encountering them; and it is not easy at first sight to distinguish the true from the false. The spurious article seems to possess all the marks of sterling quality, and to bear them bravely—often better defined than the genuine. This is not surprising, seeing that self-assertion forms part of the Somebody-character; and that quality is ever the same, whether the self-asserted superiority be good or bad, tricky or honest.

Anybody may be thought to be Somebody if he can do his fooling cleverly. We can measure the ease with which the character may be successfully assumed by the extent to which the multitude is readily duped. With what strange facility are the majority of even sensible people wont to be hoodwinked and cajoled into the surrender of their opinions and their property, their confidence, and even their affection, by the wiles of the adventurous upstart who, claiming to be Somebody, persistently and adroitly exacts a recognition he does not deserve! The convictions sacrificed, the belongings squandered, the hopes blighted, and the friendships ruined by the deceptions practised and dupes made by pretended Somebodies lie at the root of national, social, family, and personal discomfitures: hence the need of caution to detect the cheat.

The signs and tokens of truth and falseness in the parade of self-importance are not readily defined. It is easy to say that pretence is very apt to run into affectation, and that the self-assertion of a pretended Somebody is likely to be overdone. This is not the fact. He is a sorry pretender who gives himself many airs. The *rôle* of the deceiver is more likely to be one of humility and self-depreciation. The sense of *not* being Somebody then comes to his aid, and helps him in acting up to the part assumed, by checking affectation. At the same time it should be recognised that the pretender does, in a large proportion of instances, actually suppose that he is what he affects to be. After repeating a false story very frequently, a man may begin to believe it true.

Moreover, the pretender often actually becomes, after a sort, what he tries to persuade others he is. There is such a thing as converting the unreal into the real by the force of affirmation. We see this illustrated every day in the popularising of articles of commerce by skilful and persevering advertisement. Something said to be used by everybody, when it is barely known beyond the circle of its promoters, in process of time comes to be a universal necessary. In like manner Somebody who is really nobody may be made Somebody by diligent self-assertion. It is in this way that the sway of adventurous spirits over calmer minds is established. The mystery which always attends the unknown helps the achievement. A man springing suddenly from obscurity is, other things being equal, more likely to attain supremacy than one with an antecedent history that seems to augur future triumphs of popularity, if only he is clever enough to take advantage of the mystery as well as able to discharge his public duty.

The sense of self-importance rewards and inspires adventurers as well as good men, though it may come to the aid of the pretender late in his career. Whenever, and however, it comes, the feeling is real in itself, though perhaps insufficiently grounded, and it is therefore unreasonable to expect anything essentially incongruous or startling in the deportment of new men, or pretenders, which shall mark them off from the number of really important personages and brand them openly as impostors.

It is no uncommon circumstance to hear an expression of surprise that men and women not to the manner born contrive to conduct themselves even fairly well in positions of prominence. This reflection is the outcome of a mistaken mode of reasoning. It would be more startling to find that those who have proved the possession of a power to control and set aside adverse conditions had not also the wit to adapt their conduct to the positions to which they have raised themselves. The sense of being Somebody is itself educationary and elevating, and it has probably done excellent work in improving those who have experienced its influence, as well as bad work in adding plausibility to the deception practised on others. There are few things that are wholly bad, and the consciousness of superiority is not one of the number.

Nevertheless self-importance, when it dawns prematurely on a weak mind, is apt to impel the victim of its blandishments to strangely indecorous deeds and mannerisms. How infinitely grotesque is any broad affectation of superiority in station or intellect when the pretence is ill-founded! The brainless adventuress who mimics the airs of a woman of fashion; the insensate being who sets up for a person of taste without a vestige of culture; the man of money-bags who apes the man of acres—how laughably comical are the exploits of these monsters! The feeling of being Somebody is a treacherous and misleading guide, and needs to be controlled with a strong judgment if it is to be restrained from gaining the mastery over its subject and inciting him to exploits of riotous imbecility.

The vagaries and weakness of a great mind may excite pity, but they are not less ridiculous than the follies of a little mind. It may be less exasperating to be fooled by greatness than by littleness, but it is hard to tolerate the tyranny of imposture in any form, whether the offence be one of exaggerated or entirely groundless pretension. On the whole, perhaps, human nature is more inclined to condone the crime of a gross pretender than the fault of over-pretentious greatness. History tends to teach that inflated and exaggerated worth and merit have been visited with more permanent and severe chastisement on exposure than utterly hollow pretence. The latter may be almost forgiven for its audacity.

Again, the sense of importance is apt to involve its subject in disgrace by calling for the exercise of powers which he does not possess. Success in any single line of enterprise is very likely to end in this sort of disaster. A person who has achieved real excellence in one department begins to think he is Somebody, and, when he comes to play the part, fails utterly. It does not by any means follow that because a man has done something he must be Somebody. He may, or he may not. The diver does not become an aquatic animal when he accomplishes the feat of remaining under water for some seconds; and the salmon is not an air-breathing creature because it leaps above the surface, or the flying-fish a bird because he projects himself above the crest of the wave.

It is no uncommon experience for a man who has performed some feat of nobility or political genius to find himself wholly out of his element in the situation to which he has been raised, or at the work with which he has been entrusted.

It is one of the practical lessons men learn painfully in the rigorous school of experience, that the ability to perform an exceptional action does not imply the existence of power to maintain the path of supremacy achieved. The sense of self-importance may be engendered by having done something great, but it is extremely probable that it will issue in disappointment. Those are wise who keep the consciousness to themselves for a sufficiently long period to test its grounds before they proceed to give it expression in public.

Now and then we find this sense present to the mind of a man of genuine ability, and sustaining him in the doing of small things when his work and genius are, as yet, unappreciated. The feeling of power in reserve gives confidence, and it is well if it also inspires patience. There is no policy so successful as that of waiting, when the idea includes working strenuously, though unobtrusively, to a definite end. He who waits will win ; and nothing so greatly helps the self-restraint necessary to carry this policy to a full issue as a rational sense of self-importance. It arms the well-constituted mind against its own besetting impulses, it smoothes the path of privation, aids reserve, and consoles for many a passing but painful indignity.

It is not wholly, or in the main, a bad sense, this self-consciousness of fitness and capacity for better things and a higher status. The personal problem is—to use it rightly, to make it subservient to good ends, and never to let it get the upper hand or obtain the mastery. The wise man who is sensible of being Somebody in a particular sphere—and it is possible to be Somebody in any sphere—will be more intent on developing his capacity for future achievements than on hugging the consciousness for its own sake. Being really Somebody, it is little sacrifice, and no self-denial, to be unappreciated amid the associations in which the present is cast. There is no morbid discontent or sulkiness with the present, still less is there impatience, or that visionary isolation which romantic persons and impostors, alike, are wont to affect. The present is looked upon as a season of preparation, and its every opportunity is prized and utilised as means to an end—means to be made the most of, and resolutely employed to both immediate and remote advantage.

The state of mind in which inactivity is induced by the sense of being Somebody presages disappointment. The indolent and dreamy are ever prone to seek refuge from duty under the pretence of feeling worthy of better and higher things. Alas, Jonah's gourd withers too certainly! The surest proof of unworthiness is to be found in this method of expressing the consciousness. The man or woman who is possessed with the sense of self-importance, and who does not feel stirred to diligence and increased forbearance by the consciousness, is deceived. It is a convincing token of nothingness and emptiness to be without resolute purpose and lacking in energy. Such people are Nobodies, and have nothing to hope for.

——:o:——

CONSISTENCY.

THERE are few qualities more generally appreciated or less commonly understood than what we call consistency. It is one of the highest compliments which can be paid to a statesman to say that he is consistent: and in every walk of life the virtue is admired, and credit for consistency prized and coveted. Mistaking its real nature, men and women go about to imitate it. They create the semblance of certain effects which consistency is seen to produce on the general character and conduct, forgetting that, unless the fruit we covet is borne by a genuine and healthy tree it must be corrupt and unreal, however pleasant to the eye or seemingly good for food. There is something wondrously impressive in a reputation for consistency. It seems to supply the one quality needed to give the hall-marking of sterling gold to character. It imparts the stability of age to youth, and gives credit to opinions formed by a mind as yet immature. If it can be said of a man that he is consistent, that at once marks him as a person to be treated with respect even when those around him fail to understand his conduct or policy.

Consistency implies a certain continuity of action which is supposed to be impossible without principle and strength of judgment and character. A consistent person is therefore felt to be one to lean upon and look up to. The less self-reliant love to follow a leader whose policy is distinguished by this trait. The weak and wavering seek shelter under the wing of such a friend and counsellor. It seems as though, while they, poor erring mortals, are blundering and straying, the possessor of this high quality of consistency must be looking steadily far ahead, and pressing onward to the goal with undimmed vision and unhesitating step, because he walks straight before him like one who knows the way and has anticipated all its vicissitudes and difficulties. There is some truth and not a little error in this presumption.

It is possible for a clever man to earn repute for consistency without possessing the least real claim to credit for the deeper virtues of instinct and principle which the characteristic is supposed to indicate. I have no wish to depreciate the value of consistency. It is an eminently useful and, when it springs from genuine sources, a priceless quality; but, like every other good thing, it may be counterfeited, and, seeing how this particular characteristic passes current in society and among all sorts and conditions of men, it would be strange if there were not much spurious metal in the market, and seemingly excellent persons, enjoying the highest character for consistency, were not occasionally found to be tricked out in meretricious ornaments, while lacking the stability and principle that make human nature trustworthy and entitle it to confidence and respect.

Consistency of conduct is one thing, consistency of principle another. The former is only valuable as it springs from and betokens the latter. The wise will esteem the sign only so far as it indicates the thing signified. To be worth the name, consistency must be deeper than the surface. Credit is not unfrequently gained for stability of purpose by dull stupidity—a low level of intelligence that does not rise to the dignity of being moved by passing events and circumstances. Another variety of the spurious quality is that which consists simply of plasticity combined with inertia. The surrounding conditions being the same, the "creature of circumstances" is the same, and therefore seems to be consistent.

Looked at from a common-sense point of view, and with an intelligent knowledge of human nature in its manifold phases, the sameness which is often mistaken for consistency ought at once to be recognised as incompatible with that quality. A dull lifeless uniformity of opinion or conduct indicates nothing so much as insensibility; and a lack of quickness in perceiving the force of circumstances can scarcely co-exist with that high principle which is the essence and source of genuine consistency. The man who claims to be considered consistent because he thought, said, or did precisely the same thing years ago which he is thinking, saying, or doing now is asking to be credited with intense stolidity. As time rolls on, it is hardly possible that what was consistent with his age and the surrounding circumstances so long before can be consistent still.

The consistency that commands respect and inspires confidence is more than the fact—we might almost say the accident—of saying and doing the same thing again even under similar circumstances. A lump of clay and a piece of wax will assume like shapes on being thrust successively into the same mould; but the two materials have little in common beyond their plasticity. No inherent formative principle determines their configuration. Everything depends on the force acting upon them from without. They are quite as likely to take one impression as another. The form assumed by a living organism, whether a growing plant or animal, is governed by a principle incorporate in the seed and developed in the structure as it rises to maturity; external conditions may modify its details, but they can never change its nature. It is just so with the human character—the quality of consistency, which we all admire and revere, is genuine only when it springs from indwelling principle, a governing force independent of and often triumphing over the aggressive force of circumstances.

It is of the highest moment to discriminate between these widely and essentially different causes, which not uncommonly appear to produce identical results. Weak or simply pliable minds, with no mortal stamina, may, under propitious influences, long preserve an appearance of excellence and seeming strength of character because they chance to remain under the same or similar influences, but, when the outward support is removed, they yield to pressure, and display other qualities possibly antagonistic. The collapse that occurs is the simple consequence of that utter lack of real consistency too frequently illustrated in experience.

The only true consistency is that which is found

allied with *individuality* of character. There is a common error about individuality which it may be useful to mention in passing. The tendency of recent thought is to make the individual the unit of the nation, and regard the commonwealth as a mere aggregation of persons thrown together by accident, just as the members of a public company may be brought and bound together by interest. Natural relationship counts for nothing; the family has no place in the calculation. By an extension of this hypothesis individualism has come to be regarded as an isolating characteristic. A strongly-marked individuality is expected to produce egoism, if not eccentricity. This theory recognises no interdependence of intents and qualities. The individual, in his highest development, is assumed to be a man or woman capable of making way in the world by force of personal character, and most likely to be at variance with those around, being virtually independent. This is a mistaken and mischievous view of life, and one against which the young should be especially warned.

Genuine individuality is the natural development of typical qualities; the best specimen of the class is the most representative, and therefore the most closely allied with the species to which he belongs. The most perfect rose is more thoroughly a rose than one which is not so well developed. The best man or woman is more manly or womanly than others, and instead of being isolated, the individual is thrust into a prominent position as a typical and representative specimen of his order. Egoism and eccentricity are vicious traits of individual development by no means to be regarded with complaisance, or otherwise than with shame and regret.

The strength which an inherent force of consistency imparts is one that shows itself in the more vigorous growth of racial or class characteristics. Every distinctive quality springs from some latent faculty or capacity in nature. The formative force holds the individual true to his type. This is the essence of consistency—an active principle of self-respect, and self-development, which are, in fact, so many expressions of the force that determines the physical and mental characteristics of the species to which the individual belongs. Consistency is obedience to the rule of nature, subjection to the "reign of law."

There is not much virtue in the seeking of consistency as an object. When people make an effort "to be consistent," they generally fail. It is like trying to exist, or breath naturally, or to do purposely any one of a score of things which ought to be accomplished unconsciously. Thorough consistency is simple fidelity to self, and is, in fact, acting with honesty. The sort of consistency which lies in doing or saying a particular thing at one time, and long afterwards taking pains to do or say the like again, or something that will "agree" with it, is a sorry imitation of the genuine quality. If the character were properly developed, and the will were only true to itself—that is, free to follow the behests of the inner conscience—the conduct could not be otherwise than consistent. The same remark applies, and with equal force, to consistency of opinion.

If there be no guiding principle in the judgment, it is necessary to take special precautions against self-contradiction; but, if the mind is its own master, and works under the instinctive sense of responsibility and truthfulness begotten by nature, no effort can be necessary to secure consistency—that quality will be the normal outcome of healthy activity. It is astonishing what pains people take to be consistent, and how they belie themselves in the attempt. The disappointment is due to the effort; it is the penalty of trying to effect by artifice what ought to spring naturally from natural causes. No sensible man labours to be consistent in his appetite. He does not burden his memory to remember whether he likes beef or plums, and tax himself with the duty of taking or rejecting them consistently. In all his likes and dislikes he is content to leave the issue to nature. Why does not he cast the obligations of consistency in morals and policy on the same broad and strong shoulders?

The objection to this obvious course is plain to see. Man walks in a vain show; he lives for appearances; he is careful of his conduct, because it is artificial and modelled to a pattern of righteousness, instead of being the natural expression of a pure mind. Of course, if we have to keep up a pretended character for any quality, whether it be that of consistency or any other supposed virtue, we must devote time and thought to the effort; hence all the difficulty of being consistent, and hence the failure which is almost sure to occur when the attention is even temporarily diverted from the laborious task of an ideal self-impersonation.

Consistency is not worth striving for. If it is worth anything, it will come unsought. It would be too much to say that it is the highest quality, but it is certainly the surest test, of character. There is often great difficulty in distinguishing the true from the false, the pretended and artificial from the effortless and real; but, when discovered, the consistent mind is ever respectable and generally praiseworthy. It is seldom we find a person consistently bad. The natural expression of most minds is fairly innocent, if not distinguished by virtue. When therefore an individual is consistent, his conduct is generally also creditable. The aim of self-culture should be directed to the springs of action, which lie deeper than conduct. If these are pure and orderly in their working, the surface-character will be satisfactory.

Consistency implies rhythmical energy—it is the immediate effect of order. Consistent things are done, accordant opinions formed, and policy framed on the same lines of principle, because the motive forces of the character are in harmonious relation. Everything works smoothly and with precision when the head is clear and the conduct is consistent, because "the heart is right." Physicians say of the body that its functions should be performed without attracting the attention to any particular part of the organism—the effect ought to be produced while the process is unobserved. This is eminently true of the mind and character. A troubled moral organism is unhealthy. The inward struggle some persons seem to glory in is abnormal. Granted that it is caused by the conflict of good and evil impulses, these same evil forces would have been powerless to assail the better parts of man's nature if they had not been fostered in the consciousness.

Youth is the time for conquering the evil passions and uprooting the foul weeds. If this valiant husbandry is neglected, there must needs be turmoil later on in life; but the individual has himself alone to thank for the experience. Those who would be peaceful and happy in the noon-day and eventide must be up betimes and subdue the enemies of happiness, the depredators and sowers of tares. Consistency is conformity to the nature born with a man and shaped and fashioned while he is fresh and wilful.

Those who have neglected the opportunity of self-training while young can attain to the consistency which lies in governing the character only by a strong judgment founded on principle. It is never so easy to make principle an object as to develop it as an all-powerful, inspiring, and controlling force in the mind; but it is better to have principle as an object than not to have it at all. Consistency can never be made an object without counterfeiting the real quality. True consistency is unconsciously developed, and, for the most part it is unobserved by the individual by whom it is exhibited. True consistency is a thing of life, and therefore progressive. It is the growth of a feature or character, and, as the character changes, it will change, so that genuine consistency is not sameness, and does not express itself by the mere repetition of acts or words. It is consistency with the principle that underlies the conduct and determines the judgment—consistency with self. This is the only true and worthy form of the quality which all men reverence, and without which society would be unendurable, good and clear head-work impracticable, and life a continuous and cheerless toil.

——:o:——

SIMPLICITY.

It is a common practice among the least blameable, if not the most excellent, classes of society to extol the virtue of simplicity, the charm of childlike simple-mindedness. What precisely does this complicated epithet mean? In what does its essential merit and fascination consist? The stock phrases of commendation in use half a century ago glorified innocence. The fashion has so changed that this last-mentioned quality is now seldom referred to except in sarcasm. To describe a person as innocent is to impute anything but guileless characteristics.

The change is no mere alteration of terms; it signifies a variation in feeling, if not a complete revolution of thought, with respect to the features and traits of character which command respect and confidence, and win love, in a stage of moral development more advanced and calling for the display of higher and more complex qualities of heart and head to make out a claim to honest praise for purity and excellence. The time has passed when negative forms of virtue, the absence of vice, could suffice to protect the character from a pervading atmosphere, and the ever present influences, of corruption. No mere looking away from evil, turning a deaf ear to the suggestions of wrong, assuming a stolid indifference to the blandishments and allurements of wickedness, will enable a man or woman to pass uncontaminated through the crowded avenues of life under the new conditions with which existence is beset.

In old times a man could choose his associates, and it was his own fault if evil communications corrupted his nature. Now there is no opportunity for selection. The multitude presses upon us on every side; and it is no small achievement if a man succeeds in preserving any considerable share of individuality. Children are taught and trained in classes; the young of both sexes are thrown together at the most impressionable period of life. when their characters are as yet unformed, and, like soft clay, are moulded in the mass; men and women struggle together in the crush and scramble for bare existence, with no time or space for the cultivation of personal characteristics. The presence of common needs, the force of common habits, the influence of common customs and usages are irresistible, and something incomparably more potent than innocence is necessary to give that solidity and strength to the moral character which shall enable it to resist the forces, within and without, that tend to disorganise and deprave it. The instinct which discovers at once a safeguard and all-powerful preventive in the quality of simple-mindedness does not greatly err either in the appreciation of difficulties or in the recognition of forces and processes by which these may be successfully overcome.

Simplicity, or simple-mindedness, implies honesty, than which there is no more indispensable or effective element of a good and stable character. People generally have the strangest and most unsatisfactory notions imaginable about honesty. The claims of absolute probity are disregarded; the quality of perfect truthfulness is barely recognised as an active principle of morality to be realised in conduct. Persons of exemplary rectitude, animated by the highest motives, strive chiefly to conform and, for the most part, rest content with a general allegiance to the dogma of the relativity of truth which makes truth the subject of circumstances and expediency the standard of honesty. As little deception, as small a departure from a rigid line, as close adherence to the narrow and straight path, as may be possible consistently with the supposed needs of life, are regarded as a full discharge of the obligations of duty.

The low and defective estimate of personal responsibility which an incomplete perception of truth, an imperfect notion of honesty, implies takes its rise in a lack of simplicity. There is more than one object present to the mind—a double vision in place of a single picture before a single eye. Moral obliquity springs from the lack of clearness and directness in the gaze. The primary purpose to be truthful and candid—in a word, honest—is qualified by secondary considerations of prudence and a forecasting of consequences. The deep and firm hold this principle of expediency has on the judgment is proved by the ever-present thought that absolute honesty is impracticable. It is argued that, in the artificial life we lead, perfectly outspoken candour and unqualified truthfulness would lead the individual who tried to practise it a prey to the less honest folk by whom he was surrounded.

It is no doubt the fact that perfect simple-mindedness would suffer in the competition with cunning and deceit. Honesty is not the best policy in the limited and worldly sense; but it is none the less true that to be strictly truthful is, in the end, and taking the whole of life, with its debtor and creditor balance of good and evil, into account, the line of conduct which will produce the largest measure of real contentment and true happiness. Moral economists err by thinking too exclusively of the immediate market-value of such commodities as honesty. There may be times and seasons when a little clever deception, the adroit suppression of truth, the artifice of throwing a false glamour over anything which does not seem to meet the requirements of the moment, *appear* permissible. Nevertheless the policy is short-sighted; in the long run the surrender of principle brings occasion for regret, and the *finesse* is seen to have been a blunder not less than a fault. The simple-mindedness which declines these expedients is the happiest and most excellent of qualities, and in the end earns the best and the highest reward.

Another form and fruit of simple-mindedness is thoroughness. The character which is distinguished by simplicity of purpose suffers no loss of energy by the scattering of efforts. A steady gaze, a settled purpose, an unwavering earnestness, a simple motive, will carry a man rapidly and pleasantly to his goal, and spare him many troubles by the way. Instead of being diverted by the distractions and misled by the so-called temptations that allure the loiterer through life, the simple-minded worker discharges his duty, and presses forward, unaffected by the hindrances which delay less well-disposed travellers. Thoroughness is one of the priceless qualities of character and work. It enhances the value of every achievement and gives tone to virtue. Many a bitter disappointment at the end of a career might have been avoided by thoroughness at the outset and on the way. Thoroughness secures a concentration of power, so that whatever has been accomplished, however small or great the sum of the work may be, is characterised by completeness; and this, in itself, forms no inconsiderable element of perfection.

Men and women are seldom, if ever thoroughly evil; the more of thoroughness there is in a character, the greater is the probability that it will be, in the main, good. The earnestness that prompts a mind to set all its energies on a single object is generally the expression of a simple devotion to principle; and the mere fact of looking steadily at an object goes far to insure a wise judgment as to its real value. Anything which will bear the scrutiny of an earnest mind steadfastly bent upon it as an object in life is almost sure to be worthy of the time and thought bestowed upon it. The thoroughness that sometimes seems to characterise the energy of the evilly-disposed is an obstinacy which relates to an object coveted rather than a line of conduct carefully conceived and thoughtfully carried out.

The converse of thoroughness is purity; and this too is one of the striking characteristics of simple-mindedness. There is no admixture of false and true principles, because the heart is pure in its affections, and the mind clear and straightforward in its aims and purposes. Impurity is the consequence of a mingling of interests. Corruption begins at the point where the sympathies commence to wander from a single object. It may not be detected until the stream is fouled, but it is at work when desire goes out in a false direction. This is true of every form of inclination; and the wise will be warned by the first departure from that simplicity of regard and purpose which concentrates the whole of a feeling, a passion, an interest, on a single object. No man can serve two masters, and no mind can compass two objects, the same in nature, and claiming the like service, without a sacrifice of purity of intention and thought.

The estimate set upon simple or single-mindedness with purity of purpose is not commensurate with its value to the individual or to society. National character is the aggregate of personal qualities, with something superadded which grows out of association and the mutual conformative influence of opinions and policy. If individual character is uncultivated among a people, the nation cannot long be distinctive or great. If the tributary streams are polluted, the outfall will be foul. This is why it should be held to be the business of the State, in the interests of public morality, to provide for the religious instruction of the masses, and especially of the young. It is, again, a potent ground of appeal to the multitude, on the score of good citizenship, to cultivate personal integrity, in all its aspects and bearings. Simple-minded honesty and thoroughness will always attach high value to purity, and this will in no small degree conduce to the development of the virtue so esteemed.

It follows from what has already been said that there is a fourth prominent feature of simplicity—individuality. The man or woman who is honest, thorough, and pure—all of which elements of character are essentially personal—must be individualised. Nothing is so much to be appreciated in art or policy, in conduct or character, as this quality when it springs from the strength of a personal motive as contrasted with a mere affectation of eccentricity. It has been the glory of art-work in the best periods that each worker has left the mark of his tool, the impress of his individual manner and skill, on his achievements. It is the distinguishing trait of genuine excellence in all descriptions of work that the result bears token of the personal labour bestowed in its accomplishment.

This is strikingly true of the self-culture which accrues to simple-mindedness. The individual thinks and acts in obedience to an inner motive, and the momentum derived from personal impulse carries him clear of much that might otherwise mar his usefulness and deteriorate, if it did not destroy, his character. Simple-mindedness is a rare safeguard against the levelling influences that all must experience in their passage through life, and under the debilitating effect of which so many too pliable natures fall. It seems to set a fence about the moral nature and protect it alike from assault and subjugation. The sincerely simple-minded are neither offensively egotistical nor too independent, but, having a set purpose and a steady gaze on the way before them, they are less susceptible of general impressions, and the quality that individualises, spares them many a mischief and much disappointment and regret.

Simple-mindedness is innocence transmuted into an active principle—ignorance of, and insensibility to, evil — manifesting itself by a single-hearted energy expending itself upon what is good. There is an absence of *finesse*, of cunning, of low worldly cleverness, and an unhesitating devotion to something that is felt and known to be right and worthy. It is no reproach to such characters to say that they are often, perhaps generally, found associated with minds occupied with a single idea. This is not an essential consequence of the quality; but in its highest development simple-mindedness obeys the precept, "Whatsoever thy hand findeth to do do it with thy might." The labour may be varied, the achievements manifold, but for the time being he one object in view holds the gaze entranced, and the eye does not wander, nor is the spirit allowed to falter or the effort to relax. Simple-mindedness is a virtue which all should cultivate, and none more sedulously than the young and inexperienced.

One half the failures those who have trodden the longest part of their course look back upon and deplore may be justly ascribed to the lack of this quality. No amount of sagacity, no keenness of instinct, no devotion to self-interest can compensate for the want of a disposition of heart and intellect, a constitution of mind and character, which is simply intent on an object clearly discerned, and shapes its conduct in life as though no other influence sought to distract attention from the path of duty. The purity that springs from simple-mindedness has the priceless gift of *clear-sightedness*, or what is of equal value in life, faith in the ultimate triumph of right and truth and justice. "To the pure all things are pure" because simplicity of purpose pervades the whole field of vision, and whatever is not comprehended in the scope of the pure intention is disregarded.

If there be a royal road to happiness, the simple-minded find it, and the peace and contentment they participate is a boon which the vexed and scheming adventurer, however well meaning, is seldom privileged to enjoy. There is only one way in which genuine simplicity can be attained by those who would fain reap its advantages. It is compounded of the three primary qualities—honesty, thoroughness, and purity; and these produce a fourth, individuality. Those who would be simple-minded must cultivate these three virtues, and they must not shrink from the distinguishing characteristics produced.

——:o:——

THE SECRET OF A CLEAR HEAD.

THE lessons I tried to teach in the preceding papers, rightly interpreted and intelligently applied, will be found to embody the principles of healthy brain action and the secret of a clear head.

1. A sensation of heat in the head, a burning forehead, a feeling of fulness and throbbing—for the relief of which every known remedy, except the right one, is commonly tried—constitutes the premonitory symptom of dulness and confusion, the experience that alarms not less than it embarrasses a worker. If this warning sensation can be studied in the light of a general knowledge of the nature of *heat*, its mode of production, the conditions under which the temperature of an organ rises

or falls, and by what measures it may be most readily reduced, the sufferer will obtain important assistance in the task of health-*preservation*, in regard to which alone I am desirous of helping him.

2. From the study of *habit* the reader will learn to set a true value on such expertness or "cleverness" as may be acquired by practice. He will perceive that it is neither a wise nor a safe policy to trust everything to habit; that the sort of clear-headedness which consists in delegating the bulk of a task to the faculty of automatic work, thereby leaving the attention free to make a show of doing two things at once—a popular and imposing feat of cleverness—is not a great achievement or an example to be emulated. He will recognise the fallacy of the belief that "everything depends on method," adopting this term in its conventional sense. There is method in madness, and the most methodical mind may come to be the feeblest by shuffling every responsibility and difficulty on to shoulders of habit in *business*, and dissipating the power of the will by making it the idle and purposeless minister of pastime and *leisure*. The will must be strong in action and retain its grasp of the business of life, directing the mental faculties in their discharge of duty, giving steadiness to the eye, acuteness to the ear, precision to the hand, or the mind may be dis-

organised, the mental and actual vision confounded, the subjective sense of hearing disassociated from the impressions of sound, and the creature of habit find to his cost that the faculty he has too implicitly trusted with his affairs has turned upon him like a false friend or a fiend.

3. Nothing so much tends to mental disquietude as false estimates of *time*. A true measuring of the moments as they pass, a fair retrospect along the track of life and a clear far-sighted sweep of the horizon are essentials of a clear head. I have endeavoured to show how it is time, past, present, or future, seems long or short, fleet or leaden-footed, as we regard it from different standpoints and in divers moods. The sketch of this interesting subject is simply suggestive, but if it should set the mind on the right track it will not be valueless. However that may be, the subject of time-measuring is in a very obvious sense germane to the secret of a clear head.

4. The like is true of *pleasure*. Little or no good work can be accomplished unless the labourer has some measure of enjoyment in his task. It is well that he should understand the philosophy of pleasure. With a view to direct the mind to this inquiry I have thrown out a few hints.

5. *Self-importance* may range from the extreme

of vanity to that bare appreciation of self which makes life tolerable. The lesson of the review I have attempted should be that the safe and desirable development of self-consciousness in respect to capacity, merit, and worth, is that which neither depreciates too much for self-respect and confidence, nor inflates the mind with an overweening sense of being somebody; perhaps on no more solid ground than the accident of having done something which could not be repeated, or achieved a position which cannot be retained.

6. *Consistency*, as I have endeavoured to convince the reader, is a quality of the character which must be wholly natural to be of value, and can never be made an object.

7. *Simplicity* of aim and single-mindedness in conduct and policy are among the chief indications of clearness in head-work. To do one thing at a time, and that thoroughly, is a most important element of the secret we are trying to master.

Simplicity, or single-mindedness, implies and comprises integrity of purpose, thoroughness, directness of aim, earnestness, and individuality—which are the cardinal elements of "clearness" as applied to brain or head work.

To apply the principles I have endeavoured to expound is to do all man can do to ensure that greatest of personal qualifications for a useful and happy life, a sound and clear head. The motives and guiding considerations which should inspire and control the effort to attain this boon compose the secret I have tried to help the reader to find.

A CATALOGUE

OF WORKS ON

Science and Art, Natural History, General Literature.

PUBLISHED AND SOLD BY

HARDWICKE & BOGUE.

192, PICCADILLY, LONDON, W.

MAY, 1879.

INDEX OF SUBJECTS.

ACROSTICS.—One Hundred Double Acrostics. Edited by "Myself." 16mo, cloth gilt, 2*s.* 6*d.*

ALCOHOL: Its Use and Abuse. Royal 16mo, cloth, price 1*s.* *See* Health Primers, page 29.

ANGELL, H. C., M.D.

THE SIGHT, and How to Preserve It. With numerous Illustrations. Fcap. 8vo, cloth, 1*s.* 6*d.*

ANSTED, D. T., M.A., F.R.S.

THE APPLICATIONS of GEOLOGY to the ARTS AND MANUFACTURES. Six Lectures delivered before the Society of Arts. Illustrated. Fcap. 8vo, cloth, 4*s.*

BADDELEY, W. ST. CLAIR.

GEORGE VILLIERS, DUKE OF BUCKINGHAM, A Drama; and other Poems. Crown 8vo, cloth, 6*s.*

JOHN DUDLEY, DUKE of NORTHUMBERLAND. An Historical Tragedy. And Songs and Poems. Crown 8vo, cloth, 6*s.*

BARCLAY, H. D.

ORPHEUS AND EURYDICE, ENDYMION, and other Poems. With Illustrations by EDGAR BARCLAY. Crown 8vo, cloth, gilt, 5*s.*

BARETTI.

A NEW DICTIONARY of the ITALIAN and ENGLISH LANGUAGES. Compiled by J. DAVENPORT and G. COMELATI. Two vols., demy 8vo, cloth, 30*s.*

BARKER, S., M.D.

MANAGEMENT OF CHILDREN in Health and Disease: A Book for Mothers. Demy 8vo, 6*s.*

BARNARD, H.

ORAL TRAINING LESSONS IN NATURAL SCIENCE AND GENERAL KNOWLEDGE: Embracing the subjects of Astronomy, Anatomy, Physiology, Chemistry, Mathematics and Geography. Crown 8vo, 2*s.* 6*d.*

BATHS AND BATHING. Royal 16mo, cloth, price 1*s.* *See* Health Primers, page 29.

BAYLISS, WYKE.

THE WITNESS OF ART, OR THE LEGEND OF BEAUTY. With Illustrations by the Author. Second Edition. Crown 8vo, cloth, 6*s.*

BENNOCH, FRANCIS.

POEMS, LYRICS, SONGS, AND SONNETS. With a Portrait of the Author on Steel. Fcap. 8vo, cloth, 7*s.* 6*d.* A few copies on Large Paper, fcap. 4to, cloth, 12*s.* 6*d.*

BENSON, J. W.

TIME and TIME TELLERS: A Book about Watches and Clocks. With many Woodcuts. Crown 8vo, cloth, 2*s.* 6*d.*

BLINCOURT, A. de, B.E.L.

FRENCH GENDERS: An Easy Method of Distinguishing them at Sight. 8vo, 6*d.*

BONER, CHARLES.

IN THE PLAIN AND ON THE MOUNTAIN: A Guide for Pedestrians and Mountain Tourists. With Illustrations of Dress requisites, &c. Fcap. 8vo, cloth, 2*s.*

BOOK of KNOTS. Illustrated by 172 Examples, showing the manner of Making every Knot, Tie, and Splice, by "Tom Bowling." Third Edition. Crown 8vo, cloth, 2*s.* 6*d.*

BRAITHWAITE, R., M.D., F.L.S., &c.

THE SPHAGNACEÆ, or Peat Mosses of Europe and North America. Illustrated with 29 Plates. Imp. 8vo, cloth. [*In the press.*

BRANDE, Prof., D.C.L., F.R.S.L., and Prof. A. S. TAYLOR, M.D., F.R.S., &c.

CHEMISTRY. Fcap. 8vo, 900 pages, 12*s.* 6*d.*

"The best guide to the study of Chemistry yet given to the world."—*Lancet.*

BREE, C. R., M.D.

HISTORY OF THE BIRDS OF EUROPE, not observed in the British Isles. Illustrated with 238 Coloured Plates. Five vols., super-royal 8vo, cloth, £5 5*s.*; reduced price £3 19*s.*

BURBIDGE, F. W.

COOL ORCHIDS, and How to Grow Them. With Descriptive List of all the best Species in Cultivation. Illustrated with numerous Woodcuts and Coloured Figures of 13 Varieties. Crown 8vo, cloth, 6*s.*

BUSHNAN, J. S., M.D., F.R.S.

INTRODUCTION TO ICHTHYOLOGY. With 33 Coloured Plates. Fcap. 8vo, cloth, 4*s.* 6*d.*

BUTLER, SAMUEL, Author of "Erewhon."

EVOLUTION, OLD AND NEW: Being a Comparison of the Theories of BUFFON, Dr. ERASMUS DARWIN, and LAMARCK, with that of Mr. CHARLES DARWIN. With Copious Extracts from the Writings of the first three-named Authors. Crown 8vo, cloth, price 7*s.* 6*d.*

EREWHON; or, Over the Range. Fifth Edition. Crown 8vo, cloth, 3*s.* 6*d.*

THE FAIR HAVEN. Second Edition. Demy 8vo, cloth, 7*s.* 6*d.*

LIFE AND HABIT. Crown 8vo, cloth, 7*s.* 6*d.*

CAPEL, C. C.

TROUT CULTURE. A Practical Treatise on Spawning, Hatching, and Rearing Trout. Fcap. 8vo, cloth, 2*s.* 6*d.*

CARRINGTON, B., M.D., F.R.S.

BRITISH HEPATICÆ. Containing Descriptions and Figures of the Native Species of Jungermannia, Marchantia, and Anthoceros. Imp. 8vo, sewed, Parts 1 to 4, each 2*s.* 6*d.* plain; 3*s.* 6*d.* coloured. To be Completed in about 12 Parts.

CASH, JAMES.

WHERE THERE'S A WILL THERE'S A WAY; or, Science in the Cottage; being Memoirs of Naturalists in Humble Life. Crown 8vo, cloth, 3*s.* 6*d.*

CHAMISSO, ADALBERT VON.

PETER SCHLEMIHL. Translated by Sir JOHN BOWRING, LL.D., &c. Illustrations on India paper by GEORGE CRUIKSHANK. Large paper, crown 4to, half-Roxburghe, 10*s.* 6*d.*

CHANGED CROSS (THE). Words by L. P. W. Illuminated by K. K. Square 16mo, with Illuminated Crosses and Border Lines, 6*s.* *See also "Crown of Life."*

CHANGED CROSS (THE). A Large Edition of the above work, printed in outline on best Plate Paper, for Illumination. Fcap. 4to, handsomely bound, cloth gilt, 6*s.*

COLLECTION CATALOGUE for NATURALISTS. A Ruled Book for keeping a permanent Record of Objects in any branch of Natural History, with Appendix for recording interesting particulars, and lettered pages for general Index. Strongly bound, 200 pages, 7*s.* 6*d.*; 300 pages, 10*s.*; and 2*s.* 6*d.* extra for every additional 100 pages. Working Catalogues, 1*s.* 6*d.* each.

COMPANION TO THE WRITING DESK. *See "How to Address Titled People."*

CONCHOLOGY, Journal of. *See page* 31.

COOKE, M. C., M.A., LL.D.

A PLAIN and EASY ACCOUNT of THE BRITISH FUNGI. With especial reference to the Esculent and other Economic Species. With Coloured Plates of 40 Species. Third Edition, revised. Crown 8vo, cloth, 6*s.*

THE BRITISH REPTILES: A Plain and Easy Account of the Lizards, Snakes, Newts, Toads, Frogs, and Tortoises indigenous to Great Britain. Numerous Illustrations, Coloured by hand. Fcap. 8vo, cloth, 6*s.*

RUST, SMUT, MILDEW, AND MOULD. An Introduction to the Study of Microscopic Fungi. Illustrated with 269 Coloured Figures by J. E. SOWERBY. Fourth Edition, with Appendix of New Species. Crown 8vo, cloth, 6*s.*

A MANUAL OF BOTANIC TERMS. New Edition, greatly enlarged, including the recent Teratological terms. Illustrated with over 300 Woodcuts. Fcap. 8vo, cl., 2*s.* 6*d.*

A MANUAL OF STRUCTURAL BOTANY. Revised Edition, with New Chemical Notation. Illustrated with 200 Woodcuts. Twentieth Thousand. 32mo, cloth, 1*s.*

COOKE, M. C., M.A., A.L.S., et L. QUELET, M.D., O.A., Inst. et Sorb. laur.

CLAVIS SYNOPTICA HYMENOMYCETUM EUROPÆORUM. Fcap. 8vo, cloth, 7*s.* 6*d.*

COUCH, JONATHAN, F.L.S.

BRITISH FISHES. A History of the Fishes of the British Islands. Illustrated with 256 beautifully Coloured Plates. Four Vols., super-royal 8vo, cl., £4 4*s.*, reduced price £3 3*s.*

CRAWLEY, RICHARD.

THE YOUNGER BROTHER. A Comedy in Five Acts. Crown 8vo, cloth, 6*s.*

CRESSWELL, C. N., of the Inner Temple.

WOMAN, AND HER WORK IN THE WORLD. Crown 8vo, cloth, 3*s.* 6*d.*

CROWN OF LIFE (THE). By M. Y. W. With elegantly Illuminated Borders from designs by ARTHUR ROBERTSON. Uniform with "*The Changed Cross.*" Fcap. 4to, cl. extra, 6*s*.

CUVIER, Baron.

THE ANIMAL KINGDOM: Arranged after its Organisation, forming a Natural History of Animals, and Introduction to Comparative Anatomy. With considerable additions by W. B. CARPENTER, M.D., F.R.S., and J. O. WESTWOOD, F.L.S. New Edition, illustrated with 500 Engravings on Wood and 36 Coloured Plates. Imp. 8vo, cloth, 21*s*.

DARBY, W. A., M.A., F.R.A.S.

THE ASTRONOMICAL OBSERVER: A Handbook for the Observatory and the Common Telescope. Embracing 965 Nebulæ, Clusters, and Double Stars. Roy. 8vo, cloth, 7*s*. 6*d*.

DAVIES, THOMAS.

THE PREPARATION and MOUNTING of MICROSCOPIC OBJECTS. New Edition, greatly Enlarged and brought up to the Present Time by JOHN MATTHEWS, M.D., F.R.M.S., Vice-President of the Quekett Microscopical Club. Fcap. 8vo, cloth, 2*s*. 6*d*.

DE CRESPIGNY, E.C., M.D.

A NEW LONDON FLORA; or, Handbook to the Botanical Localities of the Metropolitan Districts. Compiled from the Latest Authorities and from Personal Observation. Crown 8vo, cloth, 5*s*.

DEWAR, J., L.R.C.P.E.

INDIGESTION AND DIET. Crown 8vo, limp cloth, 2*s*.

DICK, Capt. ST. JOHN.

FLIES AND FLY FISHING. Illustrated. Crown 8vo, cloth, 4*s*. 6*d*.

DRAMATIC LIST (THE). A Record of the Principal Performances of Living Actors and Actresses of the British Stage. With Criticisms from Contemporary Journals. Compiled and Edited by CHARLES EYRE PASCOE. Crown 8vo, morocco gilt, 12*s*. 6*d*. *See also page* 28.

DRURY, E. J.

CHRONOLOGY AT A GLANCE: An Epitome of Events from 4000 B.C. to A.D. 1877. With a Table giving the dates of the deaths of "England's most noted Worthies," Artists, Authors, Divines, Statesmen, Naval and Military Celebrities, &c., &c. Fcap. 8vo, sewed, 1*s*.

DUDGEON, R. E., M.D.

THE HUMAN EYE; Its Optical Construction Popularly Explained. Illustrated with 32 Woodcuts. Royal 18mo, cloth, 3*s.* 6*d.*

DUNCAN, JAMES, F.L.S.

INTRODUCTION TO ENTOMOLOGY. With 38 Coloured Plates. Fcap. 8vo, cloth, 4*s.* 6*d.*

BRITISH BUTTERFLIES: A complete Description of the Larvæ and full-grown Insects of our Native Species. With Coloured Figures of Eighty Varieties. Fcap. 8vo, cloth, 4*s.* 6*d.*

BRITISH MOTHS: A complete Description of the Larvæ and full-grown Insects of our Native Species. With Coloured Figures of Eighty Varieties. Fcap. 8vo, cloth, 4*s.* 6*d.*

BEETLES, BRITISH AND FOREIGN. Containing a full description of the more important species. With Coloured Figures of more than One Hundred Varieties. Fcap. 8vo, cloth, 4*s.* 6*d.*

NATURAL HISTORY of EXOTIC BUTTERFLIES. With 36 Coloured Plates. Fcap. 8vo, cloth, 4*s.* 6*d.*

NATURAL HISTORY OF EXOTIC MOTHS. With 34 Coloured Plates. Fcap. 8vo, cloth, 4*s.* 6*d.*

DYER, Rev. T. F. THISELTON, M.A.

ENGLISH FOLK LORE. *Contents:*—Trees—Plants—Flowers—The Moon—Birds—Animals—Insects—Reptiles—Charms—Birth—Baptism—Marriage—Death—Days of the Week—The Months and their Weather Lore—Bells—Miscellaneous Folk Lore. Crown 8vo, cloth, 5*s.*

EATON, Professor D. C., of Yale College.

THE FERNS OF NORTH AMERICA. Illustrated with numerous Coloured Plates by JAMES H. EMERTON. Demy 4to. To be completed in 20 Parts, published at intervals of about two months, price 5*s.* each.

EDGEWORTH, M. P., F.L.S., F.A.S.

POLLEN. Illustrated with 438 Figures. Second Edition, revised and corrected. Demy 8vo, cloth, 7*s.* 6*d.*

EDWARDS, A. M., M.D., C. JOHNSTON, M.D., and H. L. SMITH, LL.D.

DIATOMS, Practical Directions for Collecting, Preserving, Transporting, Preparing and Mounting. Crown 8vo, cloth, 3*s.* 6*d.*

ELVIN, C. N., M.A.

A SYNOPSIS OF HERALDRY. With 400 Engravings. Crown 8vo, cloth, 3*s.*

EXERCISE AND TRAINING. Royal 16mo, cloth, illustrated, price 1*s.* *See* Health Primers, page 29.

EYTON, C.

NOTES ON THE GEOLOGY OF NORTH SHROPSHIRE. Fcap. 8vo, cloth, 3*s.* 6*d.*

FALCONER, HUGH, A.M., M.D.

PALÆONTOLOGICAL MEMOIRS OF. By CHARLES MURCHISON, M.D., F.R.S. Illustrated. Two Vols., demy, cloth, £2 2*s.*

FERN COLLECTOR'S ALBUM: A descriptive Folio for the reception of Natural Specimens; containing on the right-hand page a description of each Fern printed in Colours, the opposite page being left Blank for the Collector to affix the dried Specimen; forming, when filled, an elegant and complete collection of this interesting family of Plants. Size 11¾ in. by 8½ in., handsomely bound, price One Guinea.

FLEISCHMANN, A., M.R.C.S.

PLAIN AND PRACTICAL MEDICAL PRECEPTS. Second Edition, revised and enlarged. On a large sheet, 4*d.*

FORBES, URQUHART A., of Lincoln's Inn.

THE LAW RELATING TO TRUSTEE AND POST-OFFICE SAVINGS' BANKS, with Notes of Decisions and Awards made by the Barrister and the Registrar of Friendly Societies. Demy 12mo, cloth, 7*s.* 6*d.*

FRY, HERBERT.

ROYAL GUIDE TO THE LONDON CHARITIES, 1878–9. Showing, in alphabetical order, their Name, Date of Foundation, Address, Objects, Annual Income, Chief Officials, &c. Sixteenth Annual Edition. Crown 8vo, cloth, 1*s.* 6*d.*

GATTY, Mrs. ALFRED.

BRITISH SEAWEEDS. Illustrated with 80 Coloured Plates, containing 384 Figures. Two Volumes, super-royal 8vo, cloth, £2 10*s.*; reduced price £1 17*s.* 6*d.*

GEACH, H. H.

A PLAIN OUTLINE OF LAW. Demy 8vo, cloth, 2*s.* 6*d.*

GEOLOGISTS' ASSOCIATION, Proceedings of. Edited by J. LOGAN LOBLEY, F.G.S. Demy 8vo, with Illustrations. Published Quarterly. Vol. I., 8 Parts, 6*d.* each; Vol. II., 8 Parts; Vol. III., 8 Parts; Vol. IV., 9 Parts; Vol. V., Parts 1 to 6, 1*s.* each.

GRANVILLE, J. MORTIMER, M.D., L.R.C.P.

THE CARE AND CURE OF THE INSANE: Being the Reports of *The Lancet* Commission on Lunatic Asylums, 1875-6-7, for Middlesex, City of London, and Surrey (republished by permission), with a Digest of the principal records extant, and a Statistical Review of the Work of each Asylum, from the date of its opening to the end of 1875. Two Vols., demy 8vo, cloth, 36*s.*

WHILE THE BOY WAITS: Essays. Cr. 8vo, cloth, 6*s.*

COMMON MIND TROUBLES. *Contents:*—Failings—Defects of Memory—Confusions of Thought—Sleeplessness—Hesitation and Errors in Speech—Low Spirits—Tempers, &c. Fifth Thousand. Fcap. 8vo, cloth, 1*s.*

THE SECRET OF A CLEAR HEAD. *Contents:*—Temperature—Habit—Time—Pleasure—Self-Importance—Consistency — Simplicity — A Clear Head. Fcap. 8vo, cloth, 1*s.*

HAMILTON, R., M.D., F.R.S.

THE NATURAL HISTORY OF BRITISH FISHES. With 72 Coloured Plates. Two Vols., fcap. 8vo, cloth, 9*s.*

The **NATURAL HISTORY** of **SEALS, WALRUSES,** &c. With 30 Coloured Plates. Fcap. 8vo, cloth, 4*s.* 6*d.*

THE NATURAL HISTORY OF WHALES and other Cetaceæ. With 32 Cold. Plates. Fcap. 8vo, cloth, 4*s.* 6*d.*

HEALTH PRIMERS. *See* page 29.

HEAPHY, THOMAS.

THE LIKENESS OF CHRIST. Being an Enquiry into the verisimilitude of the received likeness of our Blessed Lord. Edited by WYKE BAYLISS, F.S.A. Illustrated with Twelve Photographs Coloured as Facsimiles, and Fifty Engravings on Wood from original Frescoes, Mosaics, Pateræ, and other Works of Art of the first Six Centuries. Handsomely bound in cloth gilt, atlas 4to. Price to Subscribers before issue, £3 3*s.*

HIBBERD, SHIRLEY, F.R.H.S.

BEAUTIFUL-LEAVED PLANTS, NEW AND RARE. Illustrated with 54 Coloured Engravings. One Volume, super-royal 8vo, cloth, £1 5*s.*; reduced price 18*s.* 9*d.* *For First Series see under Lowe.*

HOOKER, Sir W. J., F.R.S.

SPECIES FILICUM. Being Descriptions of the known Ferns, accompanied with 304 Plates, containing numerous Figures. Five Volumes, 8vo, cloth extra, £7 8*s.*; reduced price £4.

HOOKER, Sir W. J., F.R.S., and J. G. BAKER, F.L.S.

SYNOPSIS FILICUM; or, A Synopsis of all Known Ferns, including the Osmundaceæ, Schizæaceæ, Marratiaceæ, and Ophioglossaceæ (chiefly derived from the Kew Herbarium), accompanied by Figures representing the Essential Characters of each Genus. Second Edition, brought up to the Present Time. 8vo, cloth, £1 2*s.* 6*d.*, plain; £1 8*s.*, coloured.

HOUSE (THE) AND ITS SURROUNDINGS. Royal 16mo, cloth, price 1*s.* *See* Health Primers, page 29.

HOWDEN, PETER, V.S.

HORSE WARRANTY: A Plain and Comprehensive Guide to the various Points to be noted, showing which are essential and which are unimportant. With Forms of Warranty. Fcap. 8vo, cloth, 3*s.* 6*d.*

HOW TO ADDRESS TITLED PEOPLE. With Explanations of over 500 Abbreviations, Academical, Ecclesiastical, Legal, Literary, Masonic, Imperial, and Ancient. Royal 32mo, cloth gilt, 1*s.*

HOW TO CHOOSE A MICROSCOPE. By a Demonstrator. With 80 Illustrations. Demy 8vo, 1*s.*

HOW TO USE THE PISTOL. The Pistol as a Weapon of Defence in the House and on the Road: How to Choose it and How to Use it. Crown 8vo, cloth, 2*s.* 6*d.*

HUNTER, J., late Hon. Sec. of the Brit. Bee-keepers' Association.

A MANUAL OF BEE-KEEPING. Containing Practical Information for Rational and Profitable Methods of Bee Management. Full Instructions on Stimulative Feeding, Ligurianizing and Queen-raising, with descriptions of the American Comb Foundation, Sectional Supers, and the best Hives and Apiarian Appliances on all systems. With Illustrations. Third Edition. Fcap. 8vo, cloth, 3*s.* 6*d.*

IDYLS OF THE RINK. Illustrated by G. BOWERS and J. CARLISLE. Royal 16mo, cloth gilt, 2*s.* 6*d.*

"A series of capital parodies on well-known poems, all exceedingly clever." —*Examiner.*

JARDINE, Sir W., F.L.S., F.R.S.

THE NATURAL HISTORY OF BRITISH BIRDS. With 120 Coloured Plates. 4 vols. Fcap. 8vo, cloth, 18*s.*

THE NATURAL HISTORY OF SUN BIRDS. With 30 Coloured Plates. Fcap. 8vo, cloth, 4*s.* 6*d.*

THE NATURAL HISTORY OF HUMMING BIRDS. With 64 Coloured Plates. 2 vols. Fcap. 8vo, cloth, 9*s.*

THE NATURAL HISTORY OF GAME BIRDS. With 30 Coloured Plates. Fcap. 8vo, cloth, 4*s.* 6*d.*

THE NATURAL HISTORY of PHEASANTS, PEACOCKS, &c. With 29 Col. Plates. Fcap. 8vo, cloth, 4*s.* 6*d.*

THE NATURAL HISTORY OF LIONS, TIGERS, &c. With 34 Coloured Plates. Fcap. 8vo, cloth, 4*s.* 6*d.*

THE NATURAL HISTORY of DEER, ANTELOPES, &c. With 33 Coloured Plates. Fcap. 8vo, cloth, 4*s.* 6*d.*

THE NATURAL HISTORY OF SHEEP, OXEN, &c. With 31 Coloured Plates. Fcap. 8vo, cloth, 4*s.* 6*d.*

THE NATURAL HISTORY OF MONKEYS. With 29 Coloured Plates. Fcap. 8vo, cloth, 4*s.* 6*d.*

THE NATURAL HISTORY OF BEES. With 32 Coloured Plates. Fcap. 8vo, cloth, 4*s.* 6*d.*

THE NATURAL HISTORY of the PERCH FAMILY. With 34 Coloured Plates. Fcap. 8vo, cloth, 4*s.* 6*d.*

THE NATURAL HISTORY OF THICK-SKINNED QUADRUPEDS—Elephants, Rhinoceri, &c. With 30 Coloured Plates. Fcap. 8vo, cloth, 4*s.* 6*d.*

JEWITT, LLEWELLYNN, F.S.A.

HALF-HOURS AMONG ENGLISH ANTIQUITIES. *Contents:* Arms, Armour, Pottery, Brasses, Coins, Church Bells, Glass, Tapestry, Ornaments, Flint Implements, &c. With 304 Illustrations. Second Edition. Crown 8vo, cloth extra, 5*s.*

JOHNSON, R. LOCKE, L.R.C.P., L.R.C.I., L.S.A., &c.

FOOD CHART, giving the Names, Classification, Composition, Elementary Value, rates of Digestibility, Adulterations, Tests, &c., of the Alimentary substances in general use In wrapper, 4to, 2*s.* 6*d.*; or on roller, varnished, 6*s.*

JORDAN, W. L., F.R.G.S.

REMARKS ON THE RECENT OCEANIC EXPLORATIONS, and the Current-creating Action of Vis-Inertiæ in the Ocean. With 6 Plates. Demy 8vo, cloth, 4*s.*

THE WINDS, and their Story of the World. Demy 8vo, cloth, 5*s.*

THE SYSTEM OF THE WORLD CHALLENGE LECTURES. Being Lectures on the Winds, Ocean Currents, and Tides, and what they tell of the System of the World. Second Edition. Illustrated with Maps and Diagrams. Demy 8vo, cloth, 4*s.*

THE ARGENTINE REPUBLIC, A Descriptive and Historical Sketch. Written for the Ninth Edition of the Encyclopædia Britannica. Demy 8vo, cloth, 2*s.*

KENT, W. SAVILLE, F.L.S., F.Z.S., F.R.M.S., formerly Assistant in the Nat. Hist. Department of the British Museum.

A MANUAL OF THE INFUSORIA. Comprising a Descriptive Account of all known Flagellate, Ciliate, and Pentaculiferous Protozoa. With numerous Illustrations. Super-royal 8vo, cloth.

KINAHAN, G. H.

HANDY BOOK OF ROCK NAMES. With Brief Descriptions of the Rocks. Fcap. 8vo, cloth, 4*s.*

LANKESTER, E., M.D., F.R.S., F.L.S.

OUR FOOD: Lectures delivered at the South Kensington Museum. Illustrated. New Edition. Crown 8vo, cloth, 4*s.*

THE USES OF ANIMALS in Relation to the Industry of Man: Lectures delivered at the South Kensington Museum. Illustrated. New Edition. Crown 8vo, cloth, 4*s.*

PRACTICAL PHYSIOLOGY: A School Manual of Health, for the use of Classes and General Reading. Illustrated with numerous Woodcuts. Sixth Edition. Fcap. 8vo, cloth, 2*s.* 6*d.*

HALF-HOURS WITH THE MICROSCOPE: A Popular Guide to the Use of the Instrument. With 250 Illustrations. Sixteenth Thousand, enlarged. Fcap. 8vo, cloth, plain 2*s.* 6*d.*; coloured 4*s.*

SANITARY INSTRUCTIONS: A Series of Handbills for general Distribution:—1. Management of Infants; 2. Scarlet Fever, and the best Means of Preventing it; 3. Typhoid or Drain Fever, and its Prevention; 4. Small Pox, and its Prevention; 5. Cholera and Diarrhœa, and its Prevention; 6. Measles, and their Prevention. Each, 1*d.*; per dozen, 6*d.*; per 100, 4*s.*; per 1,000, 30*s.*

LANKESTER, MRS.

TALKS ABOUT HEALTH: A Book for Boys and Girls; Being an Explanation of all the Processes by which Life is sustained. Illustrated. Small 8vo, cloth, 1*s.*

A PLAIN and EASY ACCOUNT of BRITISH FERNS. Together with their Classification, Arrangement of Genera, Structures, and Functions, Directions for Out-door and In-door Cultivation, &c. Numerous Coloured Illustrations. *A New Edition in preparation.*

WILD FLOWERS WORTH NOTICE: A Selection of some of our Native Plants which are most attractive for their Beauty, Uses, or Associations. With Coloured Illustrations by J. E. SOWERBY. *A New Edition in preparation.*

LONDON CATALOGUE OF BRITISH PLANTS. Published under the direction of the London Botanical Exchange Club, adapted for marking Desiderata in Exchanges of Specimens; and for a Guide to Collectors, by showing the rarity or frequency of the several Species. Seventh Edition. 8vo, sewed, 6*d.*

LORD, J. KEAST.

AT HOME IN THE WILDERNESS: What to Do there and How to do it. A Handbook for Travellers and Emigrants. With numerous Illustrations of necessary Baggage, Tents, Tools, &c. &c. Second Edition. Crown 8vo, cloth, 5*s.*

LOWE, E. J., F.R.A.S.

BEAUTIFUL-LEAVED PLANTS. Describing the most beautiful-leaved Plants in cultivation in this country. Illustrated with 60 Coloured Illustrations. One Volume, super-royal 8vo, cloth, £1 1*s.*, reduced price 16*s.* *For Second Series see under Hibberd.*

OUR NATIVE FERNS, AND THEIR VARIETIES. Illustrated with 79 Coloured Plates, and 909 Wood Engravings. Two Volumes, royal 8vo, cloth, £2 2*s.*, reduced price £1 11*s.* 6*d.*

BRITISH AND EXOTIC FERNS, NATURAL HISTORY OF. Illustrated with 479 finely Coloured Plates. Eight Volumes, super-royal 8vo, cloth, £6 6*s.*, reduced price £4 14*s.* 6*d.*

NEW AND RARE FERNS, NATURAL HISTORY OF. Containing Species and Varieties not included in "Ferns, British and Exotic." Illustrated with 72 Coloured Plates and Woodcuts. One Volume, super-royal 8vo, cloth, £1 1*s.*, reduced price 16*s.*

BRITISH GRASSES, NATURAL HISTORY OF. Illustrated with 74 finely Coloured Plates. One Volume, super-royal 8vo, cloth, £1 1*s.*, reduced price 16*s.*

MACGILLIVRAY, W., F.R.S.

NATURAL HISTORY of BRITISH QUADRUPEDS. With 34 Coloured Plates. Fcap. 8vo, cloth, 4*s.* 6*d.*

MANGNALL'S HISTORICAL & MISCELLANEOUS QUESTIONS. New Edition, carefully revised and brought up to the Present Time. Well printed and strongly bound. 18mo, cloth boards, 1*s.*

MARTIN, W. C. L.

The NATURAL HISTORY of HUMMING BIRDS. With 14 Coloured Plates. Fcap. 8vo, cloth, 4*s.* 6*d.*

MASON, FINCH.

MY DAY WITH THE HOUNDS, and other Stories. With numerous Illustrations by the Author. Crown 8vo, cloth.

MAUND, B., F.L.S.

THE BOTANIC GARDEN; consisting of highly-finished Figures of Hardy Ornamental Flowering Plants, cultivated in Great Britain; with their Names, Orders, History, Qualities, Culture, and Physiological Observations. Edited by JAMES C. NIVEN, Curator of the Botanic Gardens, Hull. Illustrated with 1,250 Coloured Figures. Six Volumes, super-royal 8vo, cloth, £12 12*s.*, reduced price £9 9*s.*

MICHOD, C. J., late Secretary of the London Athletic Club.

GOOD CONDITION: A Guide to Athletic Training, for Amateurs and Professionals. Fourth Thousand. Small 8vo, cloth, 1*s.*

MIDLAND NATURALIST. *See page* 31.

MILTON, J. L., M.R.C.S.

THE STREAM OF LIFE ON OUR GLOBE: Its Archives, Traditions, and Laws, as revealed by Modern Discoveries in Geology and Palæontology. A Sketch in Untechnical Language of the Beginning and Growth of Life, and the Physiological Laws which govern its Progress and Operations. Second Edition. Crown 8vo, cloth, 6*s*.

MIVART, ST. GEORGE, F.R.S., V.P.Z.S.

MAN AND APES: An Exposition of Structural Resemblances and Differences bearing upon Questions of Affinity and Origin. With numerous Illustrations. Crown 8vo, cloth, 6*s*.

MONKHOVEN, D. VAN, Ph.D.

PHOTOGRAPHIC OPTICS, including the description of Lenses and Enlarging Apparatus. With 200 Woodcuts. Crown 8vo, cloth, 7*s*. 6*d*.

MORRIS, Rev. F. O., B.A.

BRITISH BIRDS, HISTORY OF. New Edition, Enlarged. Illustrated with 365 Coloured Engravings. Six Volumes, super-royal 8vo, cloth, £6 6*s*., reduced price, £4 14*s*. 6*d*.

BRITISH BUTTERFLIES, HISTORY OF. New Edition, Enlarged. Illustrated with 72 beautifully Coloured Plates. In One Vol., super-royal 8vo, cloth, £1 1*s*., reduced price 16*s*.

BRITISH MOTHS, NATURAL HISTORY OF. The Plates contain nearly 2000 exquisitely Coloured Specimens. Four Vols., super-royal 8vo, cloth, £6 6*s*., reduced price, £4 14*s*. 6*d*.

NESTS and EGGS of BRITISH BIRDS, NATURAL HISTORY OF. New Edition, Enlarged. Illustrated with 233 Coloured Plates. Three Vols., super-royal 8vo, cloth, £3 3*s*., reduced price £2 8*s*.

NATURALIST'S LIBRARY (THE). Edited by Sir William Jardine, F.L.S. F.R.S. Containing numerous Portraits and Memoirs of Eminent Naturalists. Illustrated with 1,300 Coloured Plates. Forty-two Volumes, fcap. 8vo, cloth, gilt tops, £9 9*s*.

THE LIBRARY comprises.—**BIRDS,** 15 Vols. British Birds, 4 Vols., Sun Birds, Humming Birds, 3 Vols., Game Birds, Pigeons, Parrots, Birds of Western Africa, 2 Vols., Fly-Catchers, Pheasants and Peacocks, &c. **ANIMALS,** 14 Vols. Introduction, Lions and Tigers, British Quadrupeds, Dogs, 2 Vols., Horses, Ruminating Animals, 2 Vols.,

Elephants, Marsupialia, Seals, Whales, Monkeys, and Man. INSECTS, 7 Vols. Introduction to Entomology, British Butterflies and Moths, 2 Vols., Foreign Butterflies and Moths, 2 Vols., Beetles, Bees. FISHES, 6 Vols. Introduction and Foreign Fishes, British Fishes, 2 Vols., Perch Family, Fishes of Guiana, 2 Vols.

Fuller Details of these will be found under the authors' names. *See* BUSHNAN, DUNCAN, HAMILTON, JARDINE, MACGILLIVRAY, MARTIN, SCHOMBURGK, SELBY, SMITH, SWAINSON, WATERHOUSE.

NAVE, JOHANN.

THE COLLECTOR'S HANDY-BOOK of Algæ, Diatoms, Desmids, Fungi, Lichens, Mosses, &c. With Instructions for their Preparation and for the Formation of an Herbarium. Translated and Edited by Rev. W. W. SPICER, M.A. Illustrated with 114 Woodcuts. Fcap. 8vo, cloth, 2*s.* 6*d.*

NEWMAN, EDWARD, F.Z.S.

BRITISH BUTTERFLIES (AN ILLUSTRATED NATURAL HISTORY OF). With Life-size Figures from Nature of each Species, and of the more striking Varieties, &c. &c. Super-royal 8vo, cloth, 7*s.* 6*d.*

BRITISH MOTHS (AN ILLUSTRATED NATURAL HISTORY OF). With Life-size Figures from Nature of each Species, and of the more striking Varieties; also full descriptions of both the Perfect Insect and the Caterpillar, together with Dates of Appearance and Localities where found. Super-royal 8vo, cloth gilt, 20*s.*

The above Works may also be had in One Volume, cloth gilt, 25*s.*

NEWTON, JOSEPH, F.R.H.S.

THE LANDSCAPE GARDENER: A Practical Guide to the Laying-Out, Planting, and Arrangement of Villa Gardens, Town Squares, and Open Spaces, from a Quarter of an Acre to Four Acres. For the use of Practical Gardeners, Amateurs, Architects, and Builders. With 24 Plans. Fcap. folio, cloth, 12*s.*

NOTES ON COLLECTING AND PRESERVING NATURAL HISTORY OBJECTS. Edited by J. E. TAYLOR, F.L.S., F.G.S., Editor of "Science Gossip." With numerous Illustrations. Crown 8vo, cloth, 3*s.* 6*d.*

Contents—Geological Specimens, by the Editor; Bones, by E. F. ELWIN; Birds' Eggs, by T. SOUTHWELL, F.Z.S.; Butterflies, by Dr. KNAGGS; Beetles, by E. C. RYE, F.Z.S.; Hymenoptera, by J. B. BRIDGMAN; Fresh-water Shells, by Prof. RALPH TATE, F.G.S.; Flowering Plants, by JAMES BRITTEN, F.L.S.; Trees and Shrubs, by Prof. BUCKMAN, F.G.S.; Mosses, by Dr. BRAITHWAITE, F.L.S.; Fungi, by W. G. SMITH, F.L.S.; Lichens, by Rev. J. CROMBIE; Seaweeds, by W. GRATTANN.

PASCOE, Charles E.

SCHOOLS FOR GIRLS AND COLLEGES FOR WOMEN: A Handbook of Female Education, chiefly Designed for the Use of Persons of the Upper Middle Class. Crown 8vo, cloth, 5*s*.

THE PRINCIPAL PROFESSIONS, A PRACTICAL HANDBOOK TO. Compiled from Authentic Sources, and based on the most recent Regulations concerning admission to the Navy, Army, and Civil Services (Home and Indian), the Legal and Medical Professions, the Professions of a Civil Engineer, Architect and Artist, and the Mercantile Marine. Crown 8vo, cloth, 3*s*. 6*d*.

THE DRAMATIC LIST. *See under Dramatic, page* 9.

PERSONAL APPEARANCES IN HEALTH AND DISEASE. Royal 16mo, cloth, illustrated, price 1*s*. *See* Health Primers, *page* 29.

PHILLIPS, LAWRENCE B., F.R.A.S.

THE AUTOGRAPHIC ALBUM: A Collection of 470 Facsimiles of Holograph Writings of Royal, Noble, and Distinguished Men and Women of Various Nations, &c. Small 4to, cloth, 12*s*.

PHIN, J., Editor of American Journal of Microscopy.

HOW TO USE THE MICROSCOPE. Practical Hints on the Selection and Use of the Microscope, intended for Beginners. Second Edition. Crown 8vo, cloth, 3*s*. 6*d*.

POMONA, THE HEREFORDSHIRE. Containing Coloured Figures and Descriptions of the most esteemed kinds of Apples and Pears. Edited by ROBERT HOGG, LL.D., F.L.S. Part I. Illustrated with Coloured Figures and Woodcuts, 4to, sewed, price 15*s*.

POPULAR SCIENCE REVIEW: A Quarterly Summary of Scientific Progress and Miscellany of Entertaining and Instructive Articles on Scientific Subjects, by the Best Writers of the Day. SECOND SERIES. Edited by W. S. DALLAS, F.L.S., F.G.S. With high-class Illustrations by first-rate Artists. The FIRST SERIES, edited by Dr. HENRY LAWSON, F.R.M.S., is Complete in 15 Volumes, fully Illustrated. Price in Parts, £7 12*s*. 6*d*.; in cloth gilt, £9 2*s*.; in half morocco, extra, £11 8*s*. SECOND SERIES, Vols. 1 and 2, in Numbers, £1; in cloth gilt, £1 4*s*.; in half morocco, extra, £1 12*s*. *See also page* 31.

PREMATURE DEATH: Its Promotion or Prevention. Royal 16mo, cloth, price 1*s*. *See* Health Primers, *page* 29.

PROCTOR, RICHARD A., B.A., F.R.A.S.

HALF-HOURS WITH THE STARS: A Plain and Easy Guide to the knowledge of the Constellations; showing, in 12 Maps, the position of the principal Star-groups, night after night throughout the Year, with Introduction and a separate Explanation of each Map. Ninth Thousand. Demy 4to, boards, 5*s*.

HALF-HOURS WITH THE TELESCOPE: A Popular Guide to the Use of the Telescope as a means of Amusement and Instruction. Fifth Edition, Illustrated. Fcap. 8vo, cloth, 2*s*. 6*d*.

QUEKETT MICROSCOPICAL CLUB, Journal of the. *See page* 31.

ROBSON, JOHN E.

BOTANICAL LABELS for Labelling Herbaria, adapted to the names in the London Catalogue of Plants and the Manuals of Professor BABINGTON and Dr. HOOKER, with Extra Labels for all New Species and Varieties recorded in the recent volumes of "The Journal of Botany" and the Exchange Club Reports. In all 3,576 Labels, with Index. Demy 8vo, 5*s*.

RUSSELL, C.

THE TANNIN PROCESS. Second Edition, with Appendix. Fcap. 8vo, cloth, 2*s*. 6*d*.

SCHAIBLE, CHARLES H., M.D., Ph.D.

FIRST HELP IN ACCIDENTS: Being a Surgical Guide in the absence, or before the arrival, of Medical Assistance, for the use of the Public. Fully Illustrated. 32mo, cloth, 1*s*.

SCHLEIDEN, J. M., M.D.

THE PRINCIPLES OF SCIENTIFIC BOTANY; or, Botany as an Inductive Science. Translated by Dr. LANKESTER. Numerous Woodcuts, and Six Steel Plates. Demy 8vo, cloth, 10*s*. 6*d*.

SCHMIDT, ADOLPH, assisted by GRUNDLER, GRUNOW, JANECH, &c.

ATLAS OF THE DIATOMACEÆ. This magnificent work consists of Photographic Reproductions of the various forms of Diatomaceæ, on Folio Plates, with description (in German). Price to Subscribers, for Twelve Parts, payable in advance, £3 12*s*. To be Completed in about 25 Parts. (*Fourteen Parts are now ready.*)

SCHOMBURGK, R. H., M.D.

THE NATURAL HISTORY OF THE FISHES OF BRITISH GUIANA. With 66 Coloured Plates. Two Vols., fcap. 8vo, cloth, 9*s.*

SCIENCE GOSSIP. A Medium of Interchange and Gossip for Students and Lovers of Nature. Edited by J. E. TAYLOR, F.L.S., F.G.S., &c. Published Monthly, with numerous Illustrations. Price Fourpence, or by post Fivepence. 14 Volumes published, price 5*s.* each. *See also page* 32.

SELBY, P. J., F.R.S., F.L.S.

THE NATURAL HISTORY OF PIGEONS. With 30 Coloured Plates. Fcap. 8vo, cloth, 4*s.* 6*d.*

THE NATURAL HISTORY OF PARROTS. With 30 Coloured Plates. Fcap. 8vo, cloth, 4*s.* 6*d.*

SHARPE, W., M.D., Surgeon Army Medical Department.

MAN A SPECIAL CREATION; or, The Pre-ordained Evolution of Species. Crown 8vo, cloth, 6*s.*

THE CONQUEROR'S DREAM, and other Poems. Crown 8vo, cloth, 2*s.* 6*d.*

SHOOLBRED, J. N., Memb. Inst. C.E.

ELECTRIC LIGHTING, and Its Practical Application. With Results from existing Examples. Numerous Illustrations, crown 8vo, cloth. [*In February.*

SHOOTING ON THE WING. Plain Directions for acquiring the art of Shooting on the Wing. With useful Hints concerning all that relates to Guns and Shooting, and particularly in regard to the Art of Loading so as to Kill. By an Old Gamekeeper. Crown 8vo, cloth, 3*s.* 6*d.*

SIMMONDS, P. L., Editor of the Journal of Applied Science.

WASTE PRODUCTS AND UNDEVELOPED SUBSTANCES: A Synopsis of Progress made in their Economic Utilization during the last Quarter of a Century, at Home and Abroad. Third Edition. Crown 8vo, cloth, 9*s.*

SCIENCE AND COMMERCE: Their Influence on our Manufactures. A Series of Statistical Essays and Lectures describing the Progressive Discoveries of Science, the Advance of British Commerce, and the Activity of our Principal Manufactures in the Nineteenth Century. Fcap. 8vo, cl. 6*s.*

SMITH, Lieut. Col. C. H.

THE NATURAL HISTORY OF DOGS. With 60 Coloured Plates. Two Vols., fcap. 8vo, cloth, 9*s.*

THE NATURAL HISTORY OF HORSES. With 35 Coloured Plates. Fcap. 8vo, cloth, 4*s.* 6*d.*

THE NATURAL HISTORY OF MAMMALIA. With 30 Coloured Plates. Fcap. 8vo, cloth, 4*s.* 6*d.*

THE NATURAL HISTORY OF MAN. With 34 Plates. Fcap. 8vo, cloth, 4*s.* 6*d.*

SMITH, J., A.L.S., late Curator of the Royal Gardens, Kew.

FERNS, BRITISH AND FOREIGN: The History, Organography, Classification, and Examination of the Species of Garden Ferns, with a Treatise on their Cultivation, and Directions showing which are the best adapted for the Hothouse, Greenhouse, Open Air Fernery, or Wardian Case. With an Index of Genera, Species, and Synonyms. Fourth Edition, revised and greatly enlarged, with New Figures, &c. Crown 8vo, cloth, 7*s.* 6*d.*

BIBLE PLANTS: Their History. With a Review of the Opinions of Various Writers regarding their Identification. Illustrated with 10 Lithographic Plates by W. H. FITCH, F.L.S. Crown 8vo, cloth, 5*s.*

SMITH, WORTHINGTON, F.L.S.

MUSHROOMS AND TOADSTOOLS: How to Distinguish easily the Difference between Edible and Poisonous Fungi. Two large Sheets, containing Figures of 29 Edible and 31 Poisonous Species, drawn the natural size, and Coloured from Living Specimens. With descriptive letterpress, 6*s.*; on canvas, in cloth case for pocket, 10*s.* 6*d.*; on canvas, on rollers and varnished, 10*s.* 6*d.* The letterpress may be had separately, with key-plates of figures, 1*s.*

SOWERBY, J.

ENGLISH BOTANY. Containing a Description and Life-size Drawing of every British Plant. Edited and brought up to the Present Standard of Scientific Knowledge, by T. BOSWELL SYME, LL.D., F.L.S., &c. With Popular Descriptions of the Uses, History, and Traditions of each Plant, by Mrs. LANKESTER. Complete in 11 Volumes, cloth, £22 8*s.*; half morocco, £24 12*s.*; whole morocco, £28 3*s.* 6*d.*

SPICER, Rev. W. W., M.A.

A HANDBOOK OF THE PLANTS OF TASMANIA. Illustrated with Woodcuts and a Coloured Frontispiece. Crown 8vo, cloth, 7*s.* 6*d.*

STABLES, W., M.D.

MEDICAL LIFE IN THE NAVY. Being the Experiences of a Naval Surgeon, described for Non-professional Readers. Fcap. 8vo, cloth, 2*s.* 6*d.*

STEINMETZ, A.

SMOKER'S GUIDE (THE), PHILOSOPHER AND FRIEND. What to Smoke—What to Smoke With—and the whole "What's What" of Tobacco, Historical, Botanical, Manufactural, Anecdotal, Social, Medical, &c. Sixth Thousand. Royal 32mo, cloth, 1*s*.

SWAINSON, W., F.R.S., F.L.S.

THE NATURAL HISTORY OF THE BIRDS OF WESTERN AFRICA. With 64 Coloured Plates. Two vols., fcap. 8vo, cloth, 9*s*.

THE NATURAL HISTORY OF FLYCATCHERS. With 31 Coloured Plates. Fcap. 8vo, cloth, 4*s*. 6*d*.

SYMONDS, Rev. W. S., Rector of Pendock.

OLD BONES; or, Notes for Young Naturalists. With References to the Typical Specimens in the British Museum. Second Edition, much improved and enlarged. Numerous Illustrations. Fcap. 8vo, cloth, 2*s*. 6*d*.

TATE, Professor RALPH, F.G.S.

BRITISH MOLLUSKS; or, Slugs and Snails, Land and Fresh-water. A Plain and Easy Account of the Land and Fresh-water Mollusks of Great Britain, containing Descriptions, Figures, and a Familiar Account of the Habits of each Species. Numerous Illustrations, coloured by hand. Fcap. 8vo, cloth, 6*s*.

TAYLOR, J. E., F.L.S., F.G.S., Editor of "Science Gossip."

FLOWERS: Their Origin, Shapes, Perfumes, and Colours. Illustrated with 32 Coloured Figures by SOWERBY, and 161 Woodcuts. Second Edition. Crown 8vo, cloth gilt, 7*s*. 6*d*.

HALF-HOURS IN THE GREEN LANES. A Book for a Country Stroll. Illustrated with 300 Woodcuts. Fourth Edition. Crown 8vo, cloth, 4*s*.

HALF-HOURS AT THE SEA SIDE; or, Recreations with Marine Objects. Illustrated with 250 Woodcuts. Third Edition. Crown 8vo, cloth, 4*s*.

GEOLOGICAL STORIES: A Series of Autobiographies in Chronological Order. Numerous Illustrations. Fourth Edition. Crown 8vo, cloth, 4*s*. 6*d*.

THE AQUARIUM: Its Inhabitants, Structure, and Management. With 238 Woodcuts. Crown 8vo, cloth extra, 6*s*.

See also NOTES ON COLLECTING AND PRESERVING NATURAL HISTORY OBJECTS, *page* 19.

TRIMEN, H., M.B. (Lond.), F.L.S., and DYER, W. T., B.A.

THE FLORA OF MIDDLESEX: A Topographical and Historical Account of the Plants found in the County. With Sketches of its Physical Geography and Climate, and of the Progress of Middlesex Botany during the last Three Centuries. With a Map of Botanical Districts. Crown 8vo, 12*s*. 6*d*

TRIPP, F. E.

BRITISH MOSSES: Their Homes, Aspects, Structure, and Uses. Containing a Coloured Figure of each Species, etched from Nature. Illustrated with 39 beautifully Coloured Plates. Two Vols., super-royal 8vo, cloth, £2 10*s*., reduced price, £1 17*s*. 6*d*.

TROTTER, M. E.

A METHOD OF TEACHING PLAIN NEEDLE-WORK IN SCHOOLS. Illustrated with Diagrams and Samplers. New Edition, revised and arranged according to Standards. Demy 8vo, cloth, 2*s*. 6*d*.

TURNER, M., and HARRIS, W.

A GUIDE to the INSTITUTIONS and CHARITIES for the BLIND in the United Kingdom. Together with Lists of Books and Appliances for their Use, a Catalogue of Books published upon the subject of the Blind, and a List of Foreign Institutions, &c. Demy 8vo, cloth, 3*s*.

TWINING, THOMAS, F.S.A.

SCIENCE MADE EASY. A Connected and Progressive Course of Ten Familiar Lectures. Six Parts, 4to, price 1*s*. each. *Contents*:—Part I. Introduction, explaining the purpose of the present Course, and its use in Schools, or for Home Study.—Part II. Lecture I. The first Elements of Mechanical Physics. Lecture II. Mechanical Physics (*continued*).—Part III. Lecture III. Mechanical Physics (*concluded*). Lecture IV. Chemical Physics.—Part IV. Lecture V. Inorganic Chemistry. Lecture VI. Organic Chemistry.—Part V. Lecture VII. Outlines of the Mineral and Vegetable Kingdoms. Lecture VIII. Outlines of the Animal Kingdom.—Part VI. Lecture IX. Human Physiology, with Outlines of Anatomy. Lecture X. Human Physiology (*concluded*).

A Series of Diagrams illustrating the above has been published, a list of which may be had on application. The price of a Complete Set of Diagrams is £3; the cost of the separate sheets varies from 6*d*. to 4*s*.

"For their perspicuity, cheapness and usefulness, we heartily commend this course of Lectures to all primary schools and to very many populous localities where it is desired by influential residents to impart pleasing and instructive information free from high-class scientific phraseology."—*Journal of Applied Science.*

UP THE RIVER from WESTMINSTER to WINDSOR. A Panorama in Pen and Ink. Illustrated with 81 Engravings and a Map of the Thames. Demy 8vo, 1*s.* 6*d.*

VICTORIA INSTITUTE, or Philosophical Society of Great Britain, Journal of the Transactions of. Edited by the Honorary Secretary, Captain F. W. H. PETRIE, F.R.S.L., F.G.S., &c. Demy 8vo. Vol. XII. Part I. 7*s.* 6*d.* Part II. 3*s.* 6*d.* Vols. I. to XI., cloth, gilt tops, price £1 1*s.* each. Most of the more important articles are published also in pamphlet form. A list of these may be had on application.

VINCENT, JOHN.

COUNTRY COTTAGES: A Series of Designs for an Improved Class of Dwellings for Agricultural Labourers. Folio, cloth, 12*s.*

WAITE, S. C.

GRACEFUL RIDING: A Pocket Manual for Equestrians. Illustrated. Fcap. 8vo, cloth, 2*s.* 6*d.*

WALFORD, E., M.A., Late Scholar of Balliol College, Oxford.

PLEASANT DAYS IN PLEASANT PLACES: Notes of Home Tours. *Contents:* Dorney and Burnham—Shanklin—Hadleigh—St. David's—Winchilsea—Sandwich—St. Osyth's Priory—Richborough Castle—Great Yarmouth—Old Moreton Hall—Cumnor—Ightham—Shoreham and Bramber — Beaulieu — Kenilworth — Tattershall Tower — Tower of Essex. Second Edition. Illustrated with numerous Woodcuts. Crown 8vo, cloth extra, 5*s.*

THE COUNTY FAMILIES; or, Royal Manual of the Titled and Untitled Aristocracy of the Three Kingdoms. It contains a complete Peerage, Baronetage, Knightage, and Dictionary of the Landed Commoners of England, Scotland, Wales, and Ireland, and gives a Brief Notice of the Descent, Birth, Marriage, Education, and Appointments of each Person (in all about 11,000), his Heir Apparent or Presumptive, a Record of the Offices which he has held, together with his Town Address and Country Residences. 1,200 pages. Imp. 8vo, cloth gilt, £2 10*s.* Published annually.

THE SHILLING PEERAGE. Containing an Alphabetical List of the House of Lords, Dates of Creation, Lists of Scotch and Irish Peers, Addresses, &c. 32mo, cloth, 1*s.* Published annually.

THE SHILLING BARONETAGE. Containing an Alphabetical List of the Baronets of the United Kingdom, Short Biographical Notices, Dates of Creation, Addresses, &c. 32mo, cloth, 1*s.* Published annually.

THE SHILLING KNIGHTAGE. Containing an Alphabetical List of the Knights of the United Kingdom, Short Biographical Notices, Dates of Creation, Addresses, &c. 32mo, cloth, 1*s.* Published annually.

THE SHILLING HOUSE OF COMMONS. Containing a List of all the Members of the British Parliament, their Town and Country Addresses, &c. 32mo, cl., 1*s.* Published annually.

THE COMPLETE PEERAGE, BARONETAGE, KNIGHTAGE, AND HOUSE OF COMMONS. In One Volume, royal 32mo, cloth extra, gilt edges, 5*s.* Published annually.

WATERHOUSE, G. R.

THE NATURAL HISTORY OF MARSUPIALIA. With 34 Coloured Plates. Fcap. 8vo, cloth, 4*s.* 6*d.*

WATFORD NATURAL HISTORY SOCIETY, Transactions of the. Demy 8vo, Illustrated. Vol. I., 10 Parts, 10*s.* 6*d.*; Vol. II., Part 1, 1*s.* 6*d.*

WHINFIELD, W. H.

ETHICS OF THE FUTURE. Demy 8vo, cloth, 12*s.*

WILSON'S AMERICAN ORNITHOLOGY; or, Natural History of the Birds of the United States; with the Continuation by Prince CHARLES LUCIAN BONAPARTE. New and Enlarged Edition, completed by the insertion of above One Hundred Birds omitted in the original Work, and by valuable Notes and Life of the Author by Sir WILLIAM JARDINE. Three Vols. Large Paper, demy 4to, with Portrait of WILSON, and 103 Plates, exhibiting nearly 400 figures, carefully Coloured by hand, half-Roxburghe, £6 6*s.*

WOOSTER, DAVID.

ALPINE PLANTS. Descriptions and 103 accurately Coloured Figures of some of the most striking and beautiful of the Alpine Flowers. One Vol., super-royal 8vo, cloth, £1 5*s.*, reduced price, 18*s.* 9*d.*

ALPINE PLANTS. Second Series. Containing Fifty-four Coloured Plates, with one or two Figures on each Plate. Descriptions and accurately Coloured Figures of the most striking and beautiful of the Alpine Plants. One Vol., super-royal 8vo, cloth, £1 5*s.*, reduced price 18*s.* 9*d.*

WYNTER, ANDREW, M.D., M.R.C.P.

SUBTLE BRAINS AND LISSOM FINGERS: Being some of the Chisel Marks of our Industrial and Scientific Progress. Third Edition, revised and corrected by ANDREW STEINMETZ. Fcap. 8vo, cloth, 3*s*. 6*d*.

CURIOSITIES OF CIVILIZATION. Being Essays reprinted from the *Quarterly* and *Edinburgh Reviews*. Crown 8vo, cloth, 6*s*.

ZERFFI, G. G., Ph.D., F.R.S.L.

MANUAL of the HISTORICAL DEVELOPMENT OF ART—Prehistoric, Ancient, Hebrew, Classic, Early Christian. With special reference to Architecture, Sculpture, Painting, and Ornamentation. Crown 8vo, cloth, 6*s*.

SPIRITUALISM AND ANIMAL MAGNETISM. A Treatise on Spiritual Manifestations, &c. &c., in which it is shown that these can, by careful study, be traced to Natural Causes. Third Edition. Crown 8vo, sewed, 1*s*.

OUR ACTORS AND ACTRESSES.

"Mr. Pascoe's book of reference should have a large sale. It is a model of what such a compilation should be—full, without being tedious—impartial, accurate, and amusing. A difficult task has been well executed."—*The World.*

Crown 8vo, morocco gilt, 12*s*. 6*d*.

THE DRAMATIC LIST:

A Record of the Principal Performances of Living Actors and Actresses of the British Stage.

WITH CRITICISMS FROM CONTEMPORARY JOURNALS.

Edited by CHARLES EYRE PASCOE.

This important work contains Biographical Sketches of all the more prominent Living Actors and Actresses of the British Stage, together with Critical Notices of their performances, extracted from contemporary journals. Among the names included will be found those of JAMES ANDERSON, Mr. and Mrs. BANCROFT, KATE BATEMAN, DION BOUCICAULT, LIONEL BROUGH, J. B. BUCKSTONE, H. J. BYRON, Madame CELESTE, Mr. and Mrs. CHIPPENDALE, JOHN S. CLARKE, JOHN CLARKE, JOHN CLAYTON, W. CRESWICK, CHARLES DILLON, E. FALCONER, W. FARREN, ELLEN FARREN, HELEN FAUCIT, C. A. FECHTER, DAVID FISHER, LYDIA FOOTE, ISABEL GLYN, JOHN HARE, CAROLINE HEATH, LOUISA HERBERT, G. HONEY, H. HOWE, HENRY IRVING, DAVID JAMES, J. JEFFERSON, Mrs. CHARLES KEAN, Mrs. KEELEY, ADELAIDE KEMBLE, FANNY KEMBLE, Mr. and Mrs. KENDAL, CHARLES MATHEWS, ADELAIDE NEILSON, HENRY NEVILLE, JOHN PARRY, S. PHELPS, AMY SEDGWICK, E. A. SOTHERN, Mrs. STIRLING, BARRY SULLIVAN, EDWARD TERRY, ELLEN TERRY, KATE TERRY, J. L. TOOLE, BENJAMIN WEBSTER, ALFRED WIGAN, HERMANN VEZIN, Mrs. JOHN WOOD, and numerous others.

Demy 16mo, cloth, Price One Shilling.

HEALTH PRIMERS.

EDITORS:

J. LANGDON DOWN, M.D., F.R.C.P., HENRY POWER, M.B., F.R.C.S.
J. MORTIMER-GRANVILLE, M.D., JOHN TWEEDY, F.R.C.S.

Under this title is being issued a Series of SHILLING PRIMERS on subjects connected with the Preservation of Health, written and edited by eminent medical authorities.

The list of Contributors includes the following names:—

G.W. BALFOUR, M.D., F.R.C.P.E., J. CRICHTON BROWNE, M.D., F.R.S.E., SIDNEY COUPLAND, M.D., M.R.C.P., JOHN CURNOW, M.D., F.R.C.P., J. LANGDON DOWN, M.D., F.R.C.P., TILBURY FOX, M.D., F.R.C.P., J. MORTIMER-GRANVILLE, M.D., F.G.S., F.S.S., W. S. GREENFIELD, M.D., M.R.C.P., C. W. HEATON, F.C.S., HARRY LEACH, M.R.C.P., G. POORE, M.D., F.R.C.P., HENRY POWER, M.B., F.R.C.S., W. L. PURVES, M.D., F.R.C.S., J. NETTEN RADCLIFFE, Ex.-Pres. Epidl. Soc., &c., C. H. RALFE, M.A., M.D., S. RINGER, M.D., F.R C.P., JOHN TWEEDY, F.R.C.S., JOHN WILLIAMS, M.D., M.R.C.P.

The following Volumes are now ready:—

Premature Death: Its Promotion or Prevention.
Alcohol: Its Use and Abuse.
Exercise and Training.
The House and its Surroundings.
Personal Appearances in Health and Disease.
Baths and Bathing.

To be followed by—

The Nerves.
The Ear and Hearing.
The Heart and its Functions.
The Head.
Clothing and Dress.
Water.
Fatigue and Pain.
The Skin and its Troubles.
The Eye and Vision.
Temperature in Health and Disease.
The Throat and Voice.
Health of Travellers.
Health in Schools.
Breath Organs.
Foods and Feeding.

London: HARDWICKE & BOGUE, 192, Piccadilly, W.

PUBLISHED QUARTERLY, Price 2*s.* 6*d.*

THE POPULAR SCIENCE REVIEW:

A Quarterly Summary of Scientific Progress and Miscellany oj Entertaining and Instructive Articles on Scientific Subjects.

Edited by W. S. DALLAS, F. L. S.,

Assistant Secretary of the Geological Society.

In addition to Articles which are of abiding interest, the POPULAR SCIENCE REVIEW contains a Complete Record of Progress in every Department of Science, including:

ASTRONOMY.	GEOGRAPHY.	MICROSCOPY.
BOTANY.	GEOLOGY.	PHOTOGRAPHY.
CHEMISTRY.	MECHANICS.	PHYSICS.
ETHNOLOGY.	METALLURGY.	ZOOLOGY.

Quarterly, price 2*s.* 6*d.*; Annual Subscription (by post), 10*s.* 1c*d.*

Volumes I. to XVII. may be had, bound in cloth, price 12*s. each.*

PUBLISHED MONTHLY, Price 6*d.*

THE MIDLAND NATURALIST.

The Journal of the Associated Natural History, Philosophical, and Archæological Societies and Field Clubs of the Midland Counties. Edited by E. W. BADGER, and W. J. HARRISON, F.G.S. Demy 8vo, Illustrated. Vol. I. now ready, cloth, 7*s.* 6*d.*; Vol. II. commenced January, 1879.

PUBLISHED MONTHLY, Price 1*s.*

THE JOURNAL OF CONCHOLOGY.

Containing Original Communications, Descriptions of New Species, &c. Demy 8vo. Parts 1 to 8, 6*d.* each; Parts 9 to 17, 1*s.* each. The New (Monthly) Series commenced January, 1879.

THE JOURNAL OF THE QUEKETT MICROSCOPICAL CLUB.

Demy 8vo, Illustrated. Parts 1 to 38 (Vol. V., Part 3) are published, 1*s.* each. A few Sets of Vols. I. to IV. may still be had, bound in cloth gilt, price £2 2*s.*

London: HARDWICKE & BOGUE, 192, Piccadilly, W.

J. OGDEN AND CO., PRINTERS, 172, ST. JOHN STREET, E.C.

Published by

Facsimile Publisher
Ashok Vihar, Delhi-110052 (India)
Website: www.facsimilepublisher.com

Distributed by

Gyan Books Pvt. Ltd.
5, Ansari Road, Daryaganj, New Delhi-110002 (India)
E-mail: books@gyanbooks.com, Website: www.gyanbooks.com

2 222000 013677